St Mary Magdalene

Morning Service 1962

St Mary Magdalene

The story of Stoke Bishop Church
1860 - 2000

Roy Henderson · Keith Sheather

St Mary's PCC

First published in 1999
by St Mary Magdalene
Parochial Church Council

ISBN 0 9537370 0 4

Typeset in Times New Roman

Printed in England by J W Arrowsmith Ltd, Bristol

CONTENTS

Photographs

Most of the illustrations have been taken from the Church Archives but the authors are grateful to the following who have given permission to reproduce their photographs: Jean Higgie *(p31 baptism),* Mary Burkett *(p81 wedding),* Don Hore *(p81 fallen tree).*

Acknowledgements

The clergy in a parish and every member of the congregation ought to be aware constantly of the perspective of history. We inherit for a short time a ministry which has continued through the years and will do so long after we have departed. We can only build on what we have received. We may perhaps institute change where we believe it to be necessary but we should do it all conscious that we are part of a long history. My hope is that this book will help those who read it to appreciate all that has contributed to the present position of our parish church.

My own indebtedness in writing part of the story of Stoke Bishop church is to those who compiled the 'Memorials of Stoke Bishop' from the papers of David Wright the first vicar, and to Ron Warne, who wrote a history of St Mary's for the centenary celebrations in 1960. I would also like to thank Penny Jetzer, who sadly died before this book was completed, Mary Burkett, Pauline Nash and John Williams and the staff of the Bristol Record Office for the help they gave me in my researches and Evelyn Libra for proof reading the manuscript. I am grateful also to my co-author for his encouragement and for preparing all the materials and choosing the photos for publication.

In the nature of things the views and actions of the vicars are well recorded, which means that they tend to feature disproportionately in this book. Please remember the great contribution made to the life of St Mary's by the lay members of the congregation. Their numbers mean that only a representative few are mentioned in the text by name but without their faithful service there would have been no history at all. I hope that readers will also detect behind the story the merciful and gracious hand of our God, without whose help nothing effective could have been achieved and to whom we must give all the glory.

A.R.H.

FOREWORD
by
The Most Reverend and Right Honourable
George Carey
Archbishop of Canterbury

St Mary's will always be a very special church as far as we, and our family, are concerned. The years we spent in Bristol, Eileen's membership of the PCC, the opportunities I had to preach and lead services, the involvement of our children in Pathfinders and other young people's groups - all of these provided us with a rich experience which we still treasure today.

What is more we know that our feelings have been shared by many thousands of others since its foundation in the last century. Roy Henderson and Keith Sheather have done a remarkable job in bringing together the stories of so many and welding them into a single whole. The result is an exciting testimony to the love of God and his faithfulness to his people down the years.

Looking to the future there is much to be confident about and I look forward to seeing St Mary's go from strength to strength in the new Millennium.

+ George Cantuar

October 1999

CHAPTER ONE

1857 - 1883

The first services in St. Mary Magdalene Church, Stoke Bishop, took place in 1860, but our history has to go back a few years before that to the moment when some of those who lived in this area felt they would like to build a church and form a new parish. What motivated them to do this?

David Wright, who was to become the first vicar of this new parish tells us that "to a certain number of resident gentry, the long distance of their homes and all the surrounding neighbourhood from their parish church of Westbury-on-Trym was felt as a serious disadvantage". On the other hand William Cartwright, the vicar of Westbury on Trym, considered the plan was just a desperate attempt to help a flagging building speculation by those most likely to benefit financially from it, for in the late 1850's land was being developed for large houses in Sneyd Park. That the vicar of Westbury would be opposed to a plan which was going to remove part of his parish from his jurisdiction is not surprising. He complained that it would affect his already inadequate stipend, though when the new parish was formed he was to continue to receive the fees from weddings and funerals in Stoke Bishop, while he remained vicar of Westbury. However, he was incensed not to have been invited to a meeting when the idea of forming this new parish was first considered. The meeting took place early in 1857 at Stoke House, the home of John Battersby Harford.

John Harford owned not only Stoke House but also a considerable estate in Stoke Bishop and he was the prime mover in the formation of the new parish. He had first to persuade the Ecclesiastical Commissioners that there were sufficient funds available, not only to build the church but also to endow the living. Apart from his own contribution, by May 1858 subscribers to the new church included William Baker, who was a builder employing 160 men. He contributed £250 as well as giving the land on which the church was to be built, while gifts of £100 came from Miss Eleanore Battersby, Sydenham Teast, Thomas May, C.S. Penny and Thomas Terrett Taylor, who was described by David Wright as Mr. Harford's right hand in all that concerned the Church's interests. He and John Harford were the first churchwardens. There were others whose contributions came later, notably George Pope, James Godwin, H.V. Tebbs, John Aitken and Dr. Henry Goodeve. The doctor had retired from the East Indian Army to live in Stoke Bishop and has a road in the parish named after him. In response to the enquiry of the Commissioners, John Harford wrote that it was proposed to erect a church at the cost of £2500, that it would seat 350, and that 200 of the seats would be rented. To the question, "Does the incumbent of the parish in which the new church will be situated approve of the contemplated arrangements?" he had to answer, "No." However William Cartwright's objections did not prevent the Commissioners giving their approval to the scheme once the necessary financial requirements were assured.

The New Parish

The other requirement was that the proposed parish should have a population exceeding 300. In fact Stoke Bishop's was 554, of whom 195 were under 18 years of age and as few as 34 over 60. The area consisted of a number of large houses with well ordered estates, scattered farms and cottages, and the tiny hamlet of Stoke Bishop in the hollow with a post office, school and public house, The Three Stars. In 1853 James Martin, the owner of the Sneyd Park estate, successfully applied to Parliament for an Act to enable the land to be developed for housing. As a result large and impressive mansions were built, many by William Baker who had moved into the area from Canons Marsh. They overlooked the Gorge or the Downs and many, like those in Ivywell Road, had coach houses and stables behind them. The houses were large, and so were the households. Christopher Penny had seven children under eleven and ten servants living in. John Harford had twelve resident servants.

Following an inspection of the school in 1854, which reported that the schoolroom was too small, the foundation stone for a larger school was laid in 1856 and by 1860 there were between 70 and 80 children attending. This building, which stood off what is now Kewstoke Road, had to be enlarged after an Act of 1870 required compulsory education for children from the age of 5 to 13.

But most of the area was still fields and, in one such meadow where the cattle had grazed, the church was built. The foundation stone was laid by John Scandrett Harford of Blaise Castle on 5 August 1858 in the presence of a few family friends and connections, together with some others who lived in the neighbourhood. John Scandrett Harford, who was a close friend of both William Willberforce and Hannah More, was the uncle of John Harford of Stoke House.

Architect, Patrons and Vicar

The architect chosen to design this new church was John Norton. He had been born in Bristol and had been a pupil at Bristol Grammar School, but lived in London where he had established a large and lucrative architectural practice in both domestic and ecclesiastical buildings. Much of his church work was in the gothic style of the mid-nineteenth century. He designed the churches of Stapleton, Frampton Cotterell and Congresbury, as well as the High Cross of Bristol. Although the picture of St. Mary's when consecrated in 1860 looks very different from the Church when completed many years later, it was nevertheless part of the overall plan of John Norton which had to wait for further funds to be available before it could be fully realised.

The patrons of Holy Trinity, Westbury on Trym, were given three months in which to take up the patronage of the new living. When they did not do this, it fell to John Harford to consider who should be the first vicar. He immediately thought of the Reverend T.D. Harford Battersby, perpetual curate of Keswick, who was his brother. The latter replied that he was honoured to be asked, but felt the opportunities of his present parish, and being Rural Dean of Keswick, precluded a move to Stoke Bishop, but he offered to join his brother as one of the patrons. The patronage was kept very much as a family affair because the third patron was John Harford's brother-in-law, the Reverend Henry George de Bunsen, who was vicar of Lilleshall in Shropshire.

Thomas Battersby wrote to his sister at Stoke House that their brother John would be wise to go ahead with an invitation to the Reverend David Wright, who presumably was being considered for the living. "Because of his known character and the worth of his sermons as testified by many, it would be very desirable to secure Mr. Wright's services for the church." So David Wright, who was a Minor Canon of Bristol Cathedral at the time and 43 years of age and related to the Wright family, the well-known Bristol publishers, became the first vicar of Stoke Bishop. It is not known why the dedication chosen for the new church should have been St. Mary Magdalene, but it may be of significance that David Wright had been at Magdalen Hall (now Hertford College), Oxford.

The vicarage and its land were given by John Harford from his estate and the house stood on Stoke Hill where Eastmead Court stands now. Judging by a survey of the house in 1859 it was prone to damp, because on three sides there was no area or drainage between the external bank of earth and the walls of the house. The survey commissioned by David Wright also recommended that the entire roof be renewed. Mr. Wright was informed that he could spend up to £50 on anything that would add to his comfort. Later he described it as "a small picturesque house standing by the roadside; with its gardens, roomy stabling and coach house it covered about half an acre. In those days from the garden a widespread view was only bounded by the Welsh hills and Bristol Channel. The house had a quaint charm of its own with its bow window and outside shutters, so suggestive of a wayside inn that, though the door was not habitually standing open, there would come an inquiry from a passer-by, 'Please, do you sell beer?'" He also described it as rat infested and "admitting freely the rain", so clearly nothing had been done about the roof.

Church Services

The church when ready for consecration consisted of a nave, south aisle, small chancel and the foundations of a tower roofed over to provide a porch. The actual cost of this was £3500, a lot more than John Harford

David Wright, the first vicar

The church in 1860

had initially supposed it would be. But on 13 March 1860 all was prepared for the visit of the Bishop of Gloucester and Bristol (the two dioceses being linked at the time) for the consecration. Some members of the cathedral choir came to lead the singing of the opening hymn, 'Christ is our cornerstone, on Him alone we build.' The Bishop preached on the text, "God is spirit, and those who worship Him must worship Him in spirit and in truth." It was a day of rejoicing for rich and poor, with a gathering of the cottagers for tea being held in the school-room to celebrate the event.

There were services and visiting preachers on the four days following the consecration of the church and then David Wright preached at the two services on the Sunday. His first sermon in St. Mary's ended with these words, "May His blessing rest on all these our assemblings here; may this holy place be to us the medium of His regenerating power; may these our mortal bodies, with which we bow before our God, be raised into temples for Himself to dwell in, holier, far holier than any building made with hands; and God give us all His heavenly grace that this our earthly sanctuary shall be indeed our gate of entrance to that city above in which the apostle John saw no temple, 'for the Lord God Almighty and the Lamb were the temple thereof.'" At the second service, which was held in the afternoon because there was no lighting for the church, he preached on Acts 4 v12 and, those who heard him then and were members of the congregation throughout his 35 years as vicar, bore witness that he came back again and again to this central theme of salvation only through Jesus Christ.

Thus began the services of word and sacrament in this new parish church. Amy Elizabeth Bell, an orphan, was the first to be baptised, the service being conducted by the Reverend F.D. Maurice. He was one of the visiting preachers on the four days following the consecration of the church. At the time he was Professor of Theology at King's College, London, and founder with Charles Kingsley of the Christian Socialists, a movement which had much influence in the formation of the trade unions, co-operative societies and promoting working class education, an interesting choice as preacher for this new congregation at the beginning of its life. On the first Sunday, David Wright baptised Emily Josephine Taylor, whom he was later to describe as "emphatically a child of the church." She was confirmed when the confirmation service was first held in St. Mary's in 1875, continued to receive communion regularly, knelt as a bride to be married there, and was buried beneath the shadow of the church. Richard Dingle, a gardener, was the first to be laid to rest in the churchyard, the Vicar placing a cross of oak to mark the spot. On Easter Day in 1860 it is recorded that there were 60 communicants, 21 on Whit Sunday and 50 on Christmas Day. At this time St. Mary's was a country church, with a small sanctus bell in a turret above the chancel to call the people to worship. When it was possible to hold an evening service, and the roads and lanes were dark, many came with lanterns to guide them through the woods and over the stiles which led to the church. While some walked, Miss Dorothy Townsend recalled at the time of the church's centenary, seeing Sir Francis Tagart, who lived in a lovely house in Old Sneed Park where deer grazed on the hill side, coming to church in a carriage and pair along his private drive, now Mariners Drive.

The Building Enlarged

A growth in numbers attending services, and the raising of a further £1360 for the building fund, led to the north aisle and another vestry being added in 1864, while about this time a number of memorial windows were presented to the church, notably the great west window, the Jesse window, depicting the genealogy of our Lord, which was given in memory of Mrs. Charles Hill. The amount being given to the church in these ways has to be born in mind when one notes that the annual collections in 1863 were £249. Bishop Ellicott of Gloucester and Bristol came back and preached at the service which marked the opening of the new aisle on 20 December 1864. The old vestry became a chapel for the children until they outnumbered the capacity of the room, when it became a choir vestry, and later the churchwardens' vestry. The importance of music in the services was reflected in 1867 in the purchase of a bigger and better organ for £240, the old one being sold for £92.

After living for a few years in a vicarage that "freely admitted the rain", parishioners and friends of the Wrights contributed £2000 and a new vicarage was built on the same site and completed in 1870. Alfred George of Downside provided the greenhouse as a tribute to Mrs. Wright.

By 1871 Easter communicants had risen to 106 and the church building began to take on the appearance with which we are familiar. The church was lengthened by two bays and beyond that a west porch or narthex was added. At the same time the tower and spire began to rise. Work on the spire was nearly complete when an event took place on 20 December 1871 that it is best left to David Wright to describe in the words he spoke in church on Sunday 24 December:

> "I think it would be felt that something was wanting if this day's service were to close without a word of reference to the catastrophe which has befallen this parish in the past week, and which does, in fact, at this moment surround us. We have lost the church's ornament - an object of exceeding beauty - seen from afar - a landmark from the waters - a spectacle which distant wayfarers stopped to gaze upon with that pleasure which the beautiful must always afford. And we, who lived near it, and in a sense owned it, were come not only to admire, but many of us to love it also. It was the completion of long hopes about this church.
>
> Well, all this is gone. Caught by the blast just at the critical moment - before the perfecting of its strength was given - the supports gave way, and in the twinkling of an eye, all the fabric fell crashing to the earth in an awful overthrow. We cannot but call this disaster. We should be very wrong, however, if we called it disaster only. With the disaster there was deliverance.
>
> The ornament of the church is gone, but the church itself stands, and stands unhurt. A point or two of difference in the direction of the gust and the whole mass must have fallen upon the roof of the church, and many months must then have passed before we could have met for God's worship here again. On that ground we cannot speak of this event as disaster only. With the disaster there was deliverance. But there is a higher ground. The injury done is not past recovery; it might have been past recovery. We deem it only marvellous that no lives were lost. It was not the violence of the wind which kept the workmen from their work that day, even on the topmost planks of the highest scaffolding. But the

rain combined with the wind was too much for them. A footing on those heights was impossible. There was work to be done within the church, and the men were withdrawn to do that work. While they were there the whirlwind swept by, and the crash came. But the men were safe within the sanctuary of the church's blessed shelter. No lives were lost; no person was hurt or touched. Let us not call it disaster only - with the disaster there was deliverance. Let gratitude far outweigh lamentation - profound gratitude to Him who, in the greatness of His mercy, has averted from the building of this church a calamity, the gloom of which must have shrouded it evermore. And now we look on. The injury is not past prompt and complete recovery. In dependence on the help and grace of God I am warranted to announce, that in the fullness of its unshorn proportions, and in all its unmutilated comeliness, the spire is to rise again."

The quotation is long, but it does give an idea of David Wright's pulpit style and perhaps it is not surprising that next day, though very wet, a collection of £171 was taken towards the work of restoration. In fact the architect of the Ecclesiastical Commissioners reported that "the condition of the tower was most remarkable; not a stone had been moved; the spire must have been lifted bodily upward, doing no damage to the masonry." The Rhenish type spire, covered with tiles, and so picturesque among the trees, was safely completed in the new year.

The next requirement was a peal of bells for the tower and with the generous offer of a tenor bell from W.E. George, others were stirred into raising the sum required for the other five bells which were cast by John Taylor & Co., of Loughborough. The tenor was 3 ft. 5 ins. in diameter and weighed 13 cwts. 16 lbs. The bells were rung for the first time on 6 September 1874 and engraved on each of them are these words in Latin,

Laudate Dominum in coelis.	Praise the Lord in the heavens.
Laudate eum in excelsis.	Praise Him in the heights.
Laudate eum omnes angeli ejus.	Praise Him all his angels.
Laudate eum omnes virtutes ejus.	Praise Him all his hosts.
Laudate eum in firmamento virtutis ejus.	Praise Him in the firmament of His power.

Omnis Spiritis laudet Dominum.	Let everything that hath breath,
Alleluia.	Praise the Lord.

Alive in Word and Action

David Wright was joined in the parish by a curate, the Reverend Donald Claxton, in 1875 and he stayed for three and a half years. His vicar spoke warmly of this first in the long line of curates who served in the parish. "He seemed to stand and walk in very touch and contact with the Saviour he served. It was this which raised him and lifted him, and gave to his quiet loving service such force and power." He seems to have been very much involved with David Wright in the parochial mission that was held at the end of January 1877. There were two visiting missioners, Canon Bullock, vicar of Barrow upon Humber, and the Reverend Henry Morris, rector of Withall in Lincolnshire. The pattern of the eight day mission appears to have been frequent daily services with the missioners notable for their "fervour and devotion". Clearly there were some for whom the "peculiar excitements of the mission week" were not to their taste and two years later the question was being asked as to how far its effects had lasted in the lives of those who were emotionally affected by it. But in one way or another attempts were made to bring the gospel to the people of the parish. By Trinity Sunday 1877 sixty women were attending a monthly instruction taken by the curate on Sunday afternoons, while another Sunday afternoon each month was given over to catechising children. There were also bible classes for men.

Throughout this first period of the church's life, practical concern was shown towards those less fortunate beyond the parish boundaries. This is revealed in a list of some of the special offertories which were taken. In 1862, £35 3s 9d was contributed for the distressed cotton workers of Bristol, while later causes supported were the Bristol Ragged schools, the National Society for the Education of the Poor and Distress in South Wales. The sick were represented in offerings taken for the Bristol Infirmary and General Hospital, Home for Invalid Ladies of Clifton, Clevedon Convalescent Home and, further afield, in 1870 for the sick and wounded in the Franco-Prussian War and French Relief Fund.

In 1881 Russian families were supported with gifts and relief was sent to Bulgaria and, because of famine, to Asia Minor. There was also a special collection for Miss Leigh's Home for Young English Women in Paris.

A more considerable financial commitment was made in 1882 when, following the lead taken by four parishes in Clifton, which became affiliated with parishes in the poorer parts of Bristol, St. Mary's established a link with St. Mark's, Easton, and agreed to finance a mission curacy for part of that parish. This support continued for the next ten years. Another venture, which began around 1870, under the aegis of Mrs. Goodeve of Cooks Folly, involved the boarding out of orphans among the cottagers of Stoke Bishop. The children were allocated by the Poor Law Guardians and were welcomed into a family. In some cases the orphans were adopted by their new parents, which would mean they were taken off the rates.

End of the Beginning

The year 1883 began with the gift of a church clock. "Henry Oldland gives this clock to Stoke Bishop as a thank-offering for the mercies received during a lifetime." A short service was held on Easter Eve and, while the hymn, 'O God, our help in ages past', was sung, Mrs. Oldland went up to the clock chamber and set the pendulum in motion. As the hymn was ending the clock was striking twelve and Lent was over.

In order to explain why there is no clock face on one side of the tower, the tale is often repeated that Sir Francis Tagart, who lived at Old Sneed Park, when invited to subscribe, was told that he would be able to read the time by the church clock from his house. He is reputed to have replied that he had plenty of clocks of his own. As the owner of one of the very few houses on that side of the church and a non-contributor to the clock, it was decided not to provide a clock face for him. It is a good story, but ignores the generous nature of Sir Francis, who gave the fountain which stands in the village, and the fact that the clock was the gift of Henry Oldland, so no other subscriptions were required.

During the year a chapel was built at the end of the south aisle and the short chancel was extended. The lovely carved reredos above the Holy Table showing the supper at Emmaus is the only feature that is still there today. The arcades in the sanctuary were filled with the figures of St. James, St. John, the Virgin Mary, St Mary Magdalene, St. Peter and St. Paul painted by Mary Tothill. The three windows at the east end of the church depicted the incarnation, crucifixion and resurrection of our Lord. This final stage in the building brought the estimated cost of all to £15000, six times more than John Harford had said it would cost in his report to the Ecclesiastical Commissioners in 1858. Bishop Ellicott of Gloucester and Bristol was again invited, this time to celebrate the church's completion at a service on Sunday 4 November 1883.

Sadly in the week before this celebration Joseph Wickenden died and his funeral was held in St. Mary's. He was a prebendary of Lincoln who lived in the parish, loved the church and from its first days had helped take services and preach there. Prebendary Wickenden was a man of considerable and varied abilities, though these were hidden to some extent by his extreme modesty and diffidence. However it was his gift that provided the carvings of the scenes from the life of St. Mary Magdalene that can be seen at the top of the pillars on the north side of the church. Finally on Christmas Day 1883 lessons were read for the first time from the eagle lectern which was given by C.E.A. George, bringing to an end a particularly eventful year in the life of this parish church of Stoke Bishop.

CHAPTER TWO

1884 - 1910

If 1883 seemed to have brought to a conclusion the work of building the church of St. Mary Magdalene, Stoke Bishop, 1884 certainly saw plenty of new building in the parish. Houses continued to spring up in the area of Sneyd Park covered by the Martins Estate Act, with the smaller villas, terraced houses and shops being built in Rockleaze Road and Rockleaze Avenue. To serve this new development the Congregationalists built Christ Church on the corner of Rockleaze Avenue and Julian Road. Like St. Mary's it had a fine spire which remained a landmark in the parish until the church was demolished in 1963. But as far as the congregation of the parish church was concerned, the most important new building was to be that of the village hall.

For some time many people had felt the need of a hall in which church meetings could be held and from where the church could engage in its community work. The small room in the home of Mrs. Elizabeth Hooper, which had been used as a reading room for parishioners, was proving inadequate for this purpose. It so happened that the public house, The Three Stars, which had been run by Charles and Eliza Bevan, became vacant. When Charles Bevan died, Eliza took on the task single handed, but by 1884 it had become too much for her. This gave certain leading members of the congregation of St. Mary's the opportunity to do something they had long wanted to do, to see an end to the public house. They disapproved of it partly because coachmen seem to have spent time there while their masters and mistresses were in church and partly because it seems to have attracted people they deemed undesirable from beyond the parish. If the public house were to be demolished, it would, of course, open up an excellent site for a village hall.

The three local men most involved in this scheming were Henry Fedden, J.P., James Godwin and Sir George Edwards, J.P., who had been mayor of Bristol from 1876-9, and was to be again in 1886. Presumably it was he who was able to persuade the Bristol Corporation to pull down the public house, in spite of its being beyond the city boundary at that time and then to arrange for the land to be leased to him and his two friends, so that the three of them could become the first trustees of the village hall. The trustees had to raise the money required to erect the hall, which they did by public subscription, and the architect they employed was Henry Fedden's brother-in-law, E. Gabriel. The hall was opened on 15 October 1885 by the vicar on his birthday. It was used for parochial meetings and entertainments and provided the parish with a lending library and a place where tea or coffee could be served. The first caretaker was A. Tyler, who was also the sexton at the church. He lived in the accommodation provided above the hall.

The Children

While the village hall was being built, Stoke Bishop school was enlarged with a spacious room for the infants. The pupils of the school were expected to attend Sunday school, but there were many, even in those days, who stayed away. In 1886 out of 70 day school pupils only 36 attended Sunday school. Nevertheless at Stoke Bishop school, because of its close links with the church, the children were given a good grounding in the Christian faith. The Reverend Canon Awdry, a visiting inspector in 1892 reporting on religious knowledge, wrote, "This school has, as usual, passed a very good examination in each of the groups, testifying to much careful and efficient teaching in Holy Scripture and the catechism."

The great event of each year was the outing to Weston-super-Mare. The children of the day school and Sunday school, with teachers and many of the parents, set out from Bristol by boat in the Waverley and after a day on the sands and sampling the delights of the pier returned by boat, arriving in Bristol at about 9 p.m. We have to remember that for some this was their only excursion of the year.

The ministry of the church to children led to the formation in 1884 of the 'Guild of Samuel'. The object of the guild was to unite its

The church after its completion in 1883 still surrounded by fields

The interior was described as 'white and cold'

members in prayer and good works. The children's collections in the first year of the guild amounted to £132 and by adding money from their missionary boxes, they were able to support a child in the Girl's Orphanage in Nazareth, a child at Dr. Barnardo's Ilford Homes, and an African boy at one of the schools of the Universities' Mission to Central Africa. This was no mean achievement by the children at a time when the annual offerings in church were of the order of £700.

The vicar and Mrs. Wright had no family of their own, but it is clear that Mrs. Wright had a great love and understanding of children. There were summer parties at the vicarage, when she made exquisite little fairy wreaths from flowers, which the children then floated in saucers. In the winter there was something called 'the collecting party'. It began with prayers in the drawing room with all the children kneeling in rows and then their missionary boxes were emptied. That was followed by a tea and a present for each child. The present had to be fished for from a deep wishing-well with rod and hook from the staircase in the hall. Apart from the Sunday school there was a monthly children's service in church at 3 p.m., but one of the children records the tremendous privilege she felt it was when, at the age of seven, she was promoted to be with her mother at the 11 a.m. service.

The Easton Link Maintained

St. Mary's interest in and support for Christian mission in Easton continued and was now concentrated on the district of Eastville whose population had grown to 7000. A church was built there and dedicated to St. Thomas. Sir George Edwards had personally contributed more than £3000 towards the cost of the church and it is clear from the words of the first vicar, the Reverend T.W. Bankes-Jones, that Stoke Bishop, vicar and people, had given a great deal of money and time to further God's work in Eastville. In addition to the new church, a smith's forge had been converted into a commodious mission hall and a workmen's club was also purchased with money contributed by St. Mary's. By 1892 the parochial staff of St. Thomas, Eastville consisted of two clergy, one bible woman, and one parish nurse, who actually came from Stoke Bishop and had been introduced to the church there through the St. Mary's involvement in

Eastville. Concern for the mission of the church overseas was reflected in there being a local branch of the Church Missionary Society at St. Mary's which arranged regular lectures, often illustrated with lantern slides.

Comings and Goings

As the years passed, those who had raised the money to build St. Mary's and made up its first congregation, died one by one. John Harford died as early as 1875 and his fellow warden, Thomas Terrett Taylor, in 1880. Prebendary Wickenden's godchildren gave as a memorial to him the mosaic figures of the annunciation and the resurrection appearance to Mary Magdalene, which are in the arcades on either side of the reredos. The figures displaced by these mosaics were transferred to the chapel at the top of the south aisle and in this chapel was placed the Wickenden memorial window, to be known as the Window of the Beatitudes. Elizabeth Hooper, who not only allowed her home to be used for a reading room, but for the first 20 years had been sextoness of St. Mary's, died in 1887. By 1890 the funerals of Dr. Goodeve, P.F. Aitken, George Pope, Alfred George and James Godwin had all been held in the church, while that year William Mills Baker died in St. Mary's during a morning service. He had just sung Keble's hymn, 'New every morning is the love', so the last words in which he had joined were these,

Only, O Lord in thy dear love
Fit us for perfect rest above;
And help us, this and every day,
To live more nearly as we pray.

He laid down his book, knelt in prayer and his spirit returned to God who gave it.

By 1892, 179 people had been buried in the churchyard, but by the same year 700 infants had been baptised in St. Mary's. The numbers of children wishing to go to school necessitated a further extension to the building in 1893 when the central room was greatly enlarged. The school remained a mixed school for boys, girls and infants and catered for 235 children. The average daily attendance in 1894 was 181. For boys over thirteen the Stoke Bishop Youth Club was formed in 1893 and met in the village hall. David Wright was the first president. The boys paid three pence per month for shorthand lessons and four pence per month for leather punching. The aim of the club when it started was clearly further education and for these very practical purposes the club was open from 7 - 9 p.m. on Mondays, Wednesdays and Fridays. On Thursdays in the village hall there was an evening service. We are told that it consisted of "hearty singing and a few words of homely advice."

Parish Magazine

It is impossible to say when the parish magazine started, but it is clear that the early editions failed to pay their way and the magazine ceased to be published. In 1892 a revived magazine was produced with 130 subscribers costing two pence, double the price of its predecessor. However the following year because some people in Bristol and Redland with certain kinds of ware for sale wanted to advertise these on the back cover of the magazine, for suitable payment, the price reverted to its original one penny. The magazine was The Church Monthly, a national publication consisting mostly of cookery and gardening hints, engravings of bishops and accounts of their careers, and serialisations of improving and moral stories. There were only two pages devoted to Stoke Bishop news. In 1892 there was a report of the annual flower service when the children brought their flowers to church and in the course of the service these were arranged in the sanctuary. Afterwards at the evening service that year, when according to the vicar the congregation was the largest that had ever been present in St. Mary's, the Dean of Bristol preached for a few minutes short of an hour and was listened to with "unflagging attention." The following year there was a sad report of flowers being stolen from the graves in the churchyard. However the vigilance of one of the local police constables was rewarded when a Bristol man was apprehended and subsequently convicted of theft and fined forty shillings.

The End of an Era

David Wright, the vicar celebrated his 77th birthday in October 1894. Over the years he had had a succession of curates to assist him, but he now became convinced that the interests of the parish - temporal as well as spiritual - called for greater vigour and activity in the direction of things than, at his advanced age, he could hope to offer. However the prospect of leaving the parish where he had been vicar for thirty five years was exceedingly hard for him to bear. In a short letter to parishioners he wrote, "It has been owing to the very strength of my affection and regard for you all that the first announcement of my resignation did not come to you from myself. I could not really bring myself to inform you of the fact. And now that it is a fact, the mournfulness that it has brought into my own spirit, words of mine could not say."

In January for some years there had been an annual tea-gathering in the village hall for those Mr. Wright described as "all our cottage friends in the parish". The programme consisted of a tea followed by music and "certain cheery passages", provided by native or neighbouring talent. In 1892 this gathering had to be postponed for several weeks on account of the scarlet fever epidemic that swept through the cottage population. The following year we are told that there were 150 guests and 11 ladies presiding at the tables. Now at his final tea-gathering in January 1895 David Wright took the opportunity to remind the large numbers who had come of the importance of worship to their lives and that true fellowship, which would not be broken in this or any other world, came only through allegiance to Christ. Then on 25 January 1895 he took his final service in St.Mary's by celebrating Holy Communion on the day consecrated to the memory of his favourite saint, "the great apostle Paul".

Thus came to an end the long incumbency of David Wright. On Easter Day in 1860 there were 60 communicants. Thirty five years later the number had risen to 190. He had seen the building transformed from the small structure of 1860 to its completed size and beauty. It had been a particular joy to him that not long before his retirement, the organ had been renovated and improved. One of his concerns for the future was that the school should remain linked to the church through the continuing financial support of the congregation and not be allowed to drift into becoming a board school.

David Wright was clearly somebody who was greatly loved and respected, whose life was marked out by unaffected humility and modesty and with a tenderness for people and all God's creatures. Indeed throughout his life he did battle against cruelty to animals and against vivisection in particular. He instinctively shrank away from controversial issues and it was in his nature to avoid them if he could, but when it came to dumb and powerless creatures of God made to suffer for the supposed benefit of mankind, he confronted this evil, as he saw it, with all his energy and eloquence. However, though he felt so strongly about this, and preached upon the subject from time to time, the main thrust of his preaching was, according to the Reverend J.C. Godwin, his godson, the everlasting Father's love and our Saviour's work. There is no doubt that he was a fine preacher and that people loved to listen to him. His rural dean testified that he and many others often came to David Wright for the wisdom of his advice and counsel. He also described his sermons as learned but warm-hearted and that they both instructed and delighted those who heard them. It seems appropriate that the scenes depicted in the three stained glass windows at the east end of St. Mary's were based on memorable sermons of his.

The windows form part of the church's memorial to David Wright, for he died early in the year following his retirement. On Saturday 22 February children lined the road from his former home, while his friends from the cottages bore their vicar to the church for the funeral, and he was buried in the churchyard. The brass tablet placed in the chancel reads,

To the Memory of
DAVID WRIGHT, M.A.,
first vicar of this parish.
This tablet is erected
by his parishioners and friends
in remembrance of
his faithful ministry of thirty-five years,
his holiness and gentleness of life,
his winning proclamation of the gospel of Christ,
and his overflowing charity,
which embraced not only all men
but all the creatures of God.

He entered into rest
on Ash Wednesday, February, 19th. 1896.

The New Vicar

The trustees of the patronage had the responsibility of choosing the new vicar. As the original trustees died, those remaining were required to appoint successors and the three whose task it was to make the appointment were the Reverend E.J. Harford, vicar of Bathford, Canon Charles Wallace, vicar of Holy Trinity, Clifton, and J. Chetwood Aitken, whose house was The Glen in Stoke Bishop. The rules under which they acted required that "they look for men of blameless life, and of pure scriptural views, according to the plain sense of the Articles of the Church - full of faith and zeal. Further, they were not to appoint any person whose opinions showed any sympathy with those who would substitute forms and ceremonies for the spirit of the gospel, but to select 'proved' men, of large minds and fixed principles, whose sole aim it is to be guided by the Holy Spirit in all things, and to act for the glory of God and the benefit of their fellow creatures." They chose the Reverend Josiah George Alford, who at the time was vicar of St. Nicholas with St. Leonard, Bristol, and he accepted their invitation to become the next vicar of Stoke Bishop. He was 48 years of age.

Since his time as an undergraduate at Cambridge, Canon Alford, as he was to become when he was made an honorary Canon in 1897, had been connected with the Volunteers, and after his ordination he was gazetted chaplain of the Gloucestershire Artillery Volunteers, taking an active part in their drill and going away with them for their annual camp. When in 1898 the Territorials were inaugurated, while he was vicar of Stoke Bishop, he was appointed first class chaplain with the rank of colonel. Incidentally Mrs Alford was the daughter of a colonel in the British Army.

Perhaps the Canon's links with the military influenced his presidency of the Stoke Bishop Youth Club. He certainly introduced new rules which included no card playing, no smoking, and no whistling, and one young man was dismissed for using improper language. But alongside increased discipline, wood carving was added to the activities and boys were allowed to play chess, draughts and dominoes in the reading room. By 1898 men over eighteen were admitted to the club and the no smoking rule was relaxed, while over the next few years gradually the educational side of the club became less significant and the social side grew, with a billiard, table tennis and bagatelle room and competitions with prizes for these and other games.

Developments in School, Parish and Church

In the nation at large the Board of Education was taking a greater interest in the running of church schools. For Stoke Bishop this resulted in the school, which had been run by twenty self-appointed trustees, being now controlled by appointed foundation managers, one of whom was the vicar, ex-officio. In fact Canon Alford's interest in education was considerable and in 1903 he was invited to become a member of the Bristol Education Committee, serving this body for the next ten years.

The population of the parish continued to grow slowly, with the latest development in the Downleaze area. The 1901 census gave the population of Stoke Bishop as 1602. In 1904 the whole of the parish was taken into the City of Bristol. The residents of Stoke Bishop will have viewed this with mixed feelings. It meant that they now had to pay Bristol rates, but it also meant the provision, at last, of a proper road across the Downs from Blackboy Hill.

In the early years of the new century, a great deal of work was done to the fabric of St. Mary's. A new heating system was introduced with hot water circulating throughout the building in large-bore cast iron pipes. At the same time the aisles were re-laid with terrazzo mosaic paving. A new and larger vestry was built and the stone chancel steps were replaced with rouge royal marble. Then in 1904 an iron chancel screen was erected, being the gift of Mr. and Mrs. Charles Cruddas in memory of their four sons, all of whom died in infancy. It is difficult now to understand why this screen was ever considered suitable for the church. It was never part of John Norton's original design and detracted from the outstanding architectural feature of the arch to the choir. From the theological point of view, caging in the clergy and choir in a church built after the reformation made no sense. But it was to remain as a distinctive feature of St. Mary's until 1966.

Further additions and improvements were planned as the church prepared to celebrate its jubilee. The age of electricity had arrived and so an electric blower for the organ was purchased for £100. The church was to be lit by electricity thanks to a gift from Sir E.P. Wills. It is recorded that on 15 September 1909 the members of a committee, who were meeting in the vestry, adjourned to see the electric lights switched on and off for the first time. £250 was spent on the fabric and spire and a further £250 on the organ. This must have pleased E.A. George, who had been appointed organist and choirmaster in 1904 and continued to serve in this capacity for a further 38 years. While all this work was being carried out the church had to be closed and morning services were held in the village hall.

Spiritual Life

232 people received communion on Easter Day in 1905. On other Sundays when there were communion services at 8 a.m. and 11 a.m. there would be around fifty communicants. Some idea of the spiritual life of the church can be detected from the records of the branch of the Church of England Men's Society that was formed in 1908. Numbers were not large. There seem to have been about twelve regular members who were required to commit themselves to pray to God every day and to do something to help forward the life of the church. Members met for prayer and bible study in one another's houses and, although occasional concerts were arranged, these by no means dominated the programme. Members visited and conducted services in a home for alcoholics in Brentry and they were also concerned for the lads of Stoke Bishop whose behaviour at evensong apparently left a lot to be desired. Members discussed the problem, not in a condemnatory way, but with understanding and decided that they should try and bridge the generation gap within the church family. With this in mind they ran a weekly gymnasium class for the youngsters in the winter months.

After serving as vicar for fifteen years, Canon Alford decided to leave Stoke Bishop. At the time he seems to have had no particular job to go to, though he remained Rural Dean of Stapleton and was heavily involved with the work of church extension in the diocese. Two years after retiring as vicar, he was appointed a residentiary Canon of Bristol Cathedral. On leaving Stoke Bishop he was presented with a gift from the parishioners, a massive silver tray and a cheque for £200. In making the presentation Francis Tagart said that, "They knew that in leaving them some sphere of usefulness and activity would be open to him, and that they also knew that with his energy and ability he was not one of those who would confound leisure with idleness." Fifty years later a member of the congregation would recall with joy her participation in the croquet parties he held on the vicarage lawn, while others spoke of his cheerfulness and unconventional manner which seems to have earned him the love and respect of all who came under his care. This was especially so during the 1914-18 war, when Colonel Canon Alford worked assiduously in attending to the spiritual needs of wounded soldiers at the 2nd Southern General Hospital and at Southmead. Francis Tagart clearly knew his man.

CHAPTER THREE

1910 - 1936

When the patrons came to consider who to appoint as the next vicar of Stoke Bishop, they heard that Alfred Clifford, the Bishop of Lucknow, a Bristolian, was planning to resign and return to this country.

Born in 1849, Alfred Clifford was educated at Corpus Christi College, Cambridge, and ordained deacon in 1872 and priest in 1874. He was a curate of St. Nicholas, Nottingham, for two years before going to India with the Church Missionary Society. He was in Calcutta for five years and then at Krishnagar for six, before returning to Calcutta to be CMS secretary, combining this with the office of chaplain to the Metropolitan Bishop and in charge of the old church in the city. In 1893 the new diocese of Lucknow was formed and Alfred Clifford was chosen to be its first bishop. It needed a man of considerable strength and resource for such a position. The diocese covered an area of 106000 square miles and had a population of 50 million, including 40000 Europeans. Bishop Clifford devoted himself whole-heartedly to his task and the experience he had gained through his long residence in India proved a valuable asset. His talent as an artist was reflected in the cathedral. A wealthy American visitor to Lucknow, much impressed by the thoughtful care bestowed by the bishop and his chaplain on his wife in an illness that proved fatal, made a large donation which gave the bishop the opportunity to provide one of the most beautiful Christian churches in all India.

However after seventeen years as bishop, his health began to suffer from the strain imposed on it by the work of the diocese and he announced his intention to resign. Before his resignation took effect he was offered the living of St. Mary's and accepted it, welcoming the opportunity to return to his native city. He cannot but have been struck by the contrast between the 50 million of the diocese of Lucknow and the population of Stoke Bishop, which the census of 1911 showed to have been 1382.

As can be seen from the photo on page 31, the new vicar's appearance was very striking. His hair, which he always wore rather low on his forehead matched his splendid beard in its whiteness. He spoke quietly, with a nice choice of words and always with a sincerity based on knowledge and experience. His bearing was courteous, but zeal for the missionary cause burned deeply in his heart. The parish was indeed fortunate to have as its vicar a man of such wisdom and experience for the terrible years of the first world war. But his health in India had given some cause for alarm and he was sixty-one years of age when he arrived in Stoke Bishop.

Curates

It was customary in those days for any curate with a post in a parish to leave when his vicar retired or moved. When Canon Alford retired, the Reverend Reginald Jeffcoat, who had been with Canon Alford for four years, was fortunate to be appointed rector of Littleton on Severn. It has to be said that at this time the lot of a curate in the Church of England was far from easy. He would work for years for £120 a year and had to wait a very long time before he would be offered a living of his own. The number of curates who received no such offer, under the patronage system that existed then, was a scandal.

Six curates served in Stoke Bishop from 1890-1910. The first was Ernest Browne, who was still a curate 22 years after his ordination, with St. Mary's his fourth and last curacy. He never went on to become a vicar. John Bright was a curate in Westbury on Trym in 1866 and after three other curacies, at Stoke Bishop from 1894-5. He too never had a living. Thomas Clark was a curate for 15 years before being appointed vicar of Westwood in Wiltshire. The next curate, C.F. Doddrell, must have had some good connections because he was appointed rector of English Bicknor in the diocese of Hereford after only 5 years, while Frederick Rogers had five curacies, including his years at Stoke Bishop, and was 26 years waiting for his first living of Warmley.

Reginald Jeffcoat had been ordained in 1896, so he had been a curate for 14 years.

In his place the Reverend Roger Whytehead was appointed and apart from the four years he spent as an Army chaplain during the war, he remained curate of Stoke Bishop until 1922 and thus remained to assist Bishop Clifford throughout his entire time as vicar. He was a keen scout master and was very involved with the youth club that met in the village hall. His home, at the top end of the parish, was used for the Sunday school. In later years he became vicar of Kings Lynn and an honorary canon of Norwich and was elected Prolocutor of the lower House of Clergy in the Convocation of Canterbury in 1950. In the light of his subsequent career, it seems probable that he was one of the most capable curates ever to have served in the parish.

Character of the Parish

Some idea of the character of Stoke Bishop in the years before the first world war can be seen from the occupations of the fathers of those baptised in St. Mary's as recorded in the baptismal registers. Of the ninety different families who brought children for baptism between 1905 and 1914, nearly a third were gardeners, coachmen, chauffeurs or servants. The number of women and girls in service is not revealed, because the registers only record the father's occupation. But they do show that directors, solicitors, army officers, a surgeon, an architect, an accountant and two, who described themselves as gentlemen, made up only 10 per cent. The rural nature of the parish was reflected in two farm labourers and a shepherd, and two dairymen, while other jobs represented include two station masters and a GWR guard, a carter, two masons, two coal merchants and a corn merchant and two sergeants, one of police and the other of the army. The full list can be seen in Appendix 4 and makes an interesting comparison with the occupations fifty years later of a similar number who brought their children for baptism in 1958 and the first months of 1959. (Appendix 5).

Ethel Griffin Watkins tells of her time at Stoke Bishop school in the days before the first world war. The school under its headmaster, Tom Miller, must have had a good reputation because children walked to the school from as far away as Shirehampton and Westbury on Trym. There were no school buses and the boys who learnt swimming had to walk to the Kingsdown baths, while the girls had to walk across the Downs in all weathers for cookery classes at Anglesea Place school at the bottom of Blackboy Hill.

Each year there were three great occasions at the school - St. George's Day when the children sang a special song, 'Flag of Britain proudly waving over distant seas', the day in July when they boarded the pleasure steamer Britannia at Hotwells for a day at Weston-super-Mare and the day when the school broke up for Christmas and a huge table draped with the Union Jack was laden with books, boxes of paints and needlework cases, which were the prizes awarded for work in the past year. Those children who had attended without an absent mark were privileged to wear a laurel wreath which had been made by senior girls a few days earlier. Special songs and recitations had been learnt for the occasion, which was attended by the governors, and two Stoke Bishop ladies gave each child an orange and a large bun as they filed out.

In 1912 the sanctuary of the parish church was decorated by Major Francis and Lt. Col. H.Tagart in memory of their parents, Sir Francis and Lady Tagart and, following the decoration, the sanctuary took on the appearance with which we are familiar, though the woodwork of the ceiling retained its dark brown colour. But with the first world war intervening it was ten years before any further improvements were made to the church building.

The War Years

On the Sunday after the outbreak of war, the service registers indicate that the vicar preached on the text, "God is our refuge and strength, a very present help in trouble." It is unlikely that anyone there could envisage the trouble that would come to so many in the parish in the next four years. The names of sixty-two young men from Stoke Bishop who died in battle would be recorded on the war memorial. Three families each lost three sons, and one of these was that of Mrs Nott, who was a widow and lived at Stoke House. Capt. Peter Nott was killed in 1916, while Capt. Cameron Nott and Lt.Col. T.W.Nott died in the battles of 1917. Ethel

Watkins recalled the very poignant moment when the school roll of honour was dedicated by Bishop Clifford in the church. "As each name was read out, Mr. Miller, our master - as we called him - wept unashamedly." Sadly the school bronze plaque on which the names were engraved was destroyed when incendiary bombs landed on the school during the second world war.

Throughout the war intercessions were held on Wednesday evenings at 8 p.m. or at 12 noon in the winter. There is no record of how many attended, but on Easter Day in 1916 there were 99 communicants at 7 a.m., 86 at 8 a.m. and a further 65 at 11 a.m., making a total for the day of 250. Bishop Clifford was naturally involved in visiting bereaved families, as well as the wounded who were in a hospital opened at Bishops Knoll.

The owner of The Knoll was Robert ('Colonel') Bush. As a boy he had been educated at Clifton College, but he left Bristol for Australia where he made a fortune sheep farming. He returned to Bristol and purchased The Knoll, in which home he and his wife raised a large family. The house itself boasted a fine entrance hall panelled in dark oak leading through to a large conservatory, called the winter garden. There was a Chinese room, a billiard room and a ballroom which contained a stage. Within the grounds there was a tennis court, a timber table-tennis chalet and, to the north of today's Bramble Lane, a horseriding exercise ground. During the war, in gratitude for his good fortune in Australia, Robert Bush converted this splendid house into a 100-bed hospital for wounded Australian soldiers, while he and his family moved to a neighbouring house called The Oak. There in the hospital great care was taken in providing every means for the recuperation of the men and it is recorded that "Bishop Clifford's gracious, dignified and helpful presence ministered to and cheered the men who were nursed there." The care given at this hospital was remembered with gratitude by many Australians, who when they came to this country years later revisited the house and a commemorative plaque was presented by the soldiers to their hosts at the end of the war. When the house was demolished in 1972, this plaque was taken to Australia and installed in the War Museum in Canberra.

During the war Stoke Bishop also became the home for some refugee families from Belgium. In all there were some fifty of them resident in the parish and the Belgian men were invited to use the village hall and club. When at last the armistice was signed on 11 November 1918, the vicar took as his text on the following Sunday, Psalm 98 v 1, "O sing unto the Lord a new song, for He hath done marvellous things."

The War Memorial Cross recording the names of those who died in the 1914-18 war was dedicated by the Bishop of Bristol in May 1920 and an endowment fund raised a sum of £100 which was placed in the care of the Society of Merchant Venturers, the income from the investment to be used by the parish to maintain the Cross in good repair.

A house opposite the village hall was purchased for a men's club in memory of those who had died and to provide a place of recreation for those who returned from the war. It was a nice idea, but ten years later very few men went there to play billiards. The cost of maintaining the club was too much for an impoverished village hall committee, so it was let as a private house and then sold in 1935. Another memorial that has lasted and has added so much to the attractiveness of St. Mary's is the Lych Gate at the Mariner's Drive entrance to the churchyard. It was erected in memory of two young men killed in action in 1918, Lt. L.H. Fry, aged 25, and Lt. A.C. Strachan, M.C., aged 23, and dedicated on 12 December 1919. Within the church there is a prayer desk given in memory of Burnet James by his parents. He was killed in action in 1915.

The Government of the Church

During the war, clergy at home and chaplains with the forces were anxious that when the war ended the church should be able to go forward with new vigour to reform itself and so be more able to meet the needs of the new world. As soon as the war was over plans were drawn up for a new system of church government. For years there had been crippling delays to all legislation with respect to the Church of England because parliament had been unable to devote time to its debate and consideration. At the same time the management of the affairs of a parish church had been in the sole hands of the vicar and churchwardens. The basis for the new scheme was a church electoral roll in each parish and, while some advocated that only communicants should be admitted to this roll, it was eventually decided that membership should be allowed for all who "are

Josiah Alford
1895-1909

Alfred Clifford
1910-1921

Fred Norton
1921-1936

16 July 1921. Four officers from the 6th Glo'sters and their wives outside St Mary's after the joint baptism of their babies all born in 1921

From Left to Right: ***Captain Peter and Mrs Lowicke, Captain and Mrs Calvert-Fisher, the Bishop of Bristol (presiding), Lieutenant William and Mrs King, Major Thomas and Mrs Lennard.***

baptised and declare that they are members of the Church of England and do not belong to any religious body which is not in communion with the Church of England."

Having established this wide democratic base, the Parliamentary Bill went on to set up a number of elected bodies, the Parochial Church Council, Ruridecanal and Diocesan Conferences and, the National Assembly of the Church of England. The 'Enabling Act', as it came to be called, was passed by Parliament in December 1919 and in our parish the electoral roll was compiled. There is no record of the number on this first electoral roll, but in 1922 there were 455 on the church electoral roll out of a total population in the parish of 1449. The first meeting of the newly elected Parochial Church Council was held in the vicarage on 16 April 1920.

This first meeting, with Bishop Clifford in the chair, opened with prayer and then the vicar spoke of the importance of preserving a spiritual atmosphere in all the deliberations of the council. It was agreed that they should meet at least once a quarter and that at a future meeting they should discuss the best ways of securing more hearty and reverent congregational worship in the church services. After discussion at the next meeting, they agreed to arrange for a congregational practice of the hymns and psalms and to ask the organist to transpose the tunes if he felt they were pitched too high. In these early meetings of the council sub-committees were formed to deal with finance, mission, the parish magazine and the Sunday schools. The latter were held in the village hall and the curate's house in Downleaze. And inevitably time was spent considering how best to raise money for the diocesan quota which had been doubled from £100 to £200 in 1920.

The Changes in Stoke Bishop

Following the death of Mrs. Clifford, the vicar announced at a PCC meeting on 12 January 1921, his intention to resign. It later emerged that throughout his time at St. Mary's, Bishop Clifford had never retained the vicar's fees for weddings and funerals and thus had made a considerable contribution to parochial funds over the years. When he relinquished office in April 1921 he was in his seventy-first year. He lived for a further ten years and was buried in Henbury churchyard.

The new vicar chosen by the patrons was the Reverend Fred Norton, who came to Stoke Bishop having previously been both curate and vicar of St. Mary the Virgin, Tyndall's Park. He had the reputation of being an expert footballer, golfer and cartoonist. He was made an Honorary Canon of Bristol Cathedral in 1924 and during his time as vicar he saw the development of Stoke Bishop from a quiet village on the edge of Bristol to a residential suburb of the city.

The first stage in the development began in 1926. A new stretch of road had been made from the village hall to what is now Glen Drive and this was followed by the building of houses on Druid Road and parts of Old Sneed Road and Old Sneed Avenue. In the 1930's building plots were being purchased and houses built in Kewstoke Road, Cranleigh Gardens, Little Stoke Road, Ormerod Road and the surrounding areas. Development continued in the remaining parts of Old Sneed Road and The Avenue, as well as Druid Hill, while nearer the church the 'Stride' estate was built with new houses in Church Road, Old Sneed Park and along Mariners Drive. In the centre of the village, after the Post Office corner had been built, the Glen, a Georgian house, was demolished, so that shops could be built to supply the needs of the growing population. These were opened in 1935.

In the twenties two significant changes were made to the fabric of St. Mary's. In November 1922 the vicar received the following letter from Sir Edward James, of Springfort, and a former Lord Mayor of Bristol. "As you know, for some time my wife and I, - and we know that other parishioners are of the same opinion - have thought the south chapel of our parish church in its present state hardly worthy of the services for which it is now needed. With this in view, we recently consulted the eminent ecclesiastical architect, Mr. J.N. Comper, as to what he would advise done to it. He has sent us his suggestions in the form of plans, which we have discussed together on two or three occasions. I am now sending you the plans, and should be obliged if you would submit them to our parochial church council. Should they approve .... we ourselves shall be pleased to carry out what Mr. Comper recommends, as a thank-offering for many blessings we have received." Sir Edward went on to say that Mrs. Wright, the widow of the first vicar, approved the plans.

The PCC unanimously carried a motion expressing appreciation of the plans and the generous offer of Sir Edward and Lady James, and authorised the vicar to apply for the necessary faculty. Our chapel was thus one of the early examples of the work of Sir Ninian Comper, as he was to become, and the Holy Table, reredos, panelling and screen for what became known as the James Chapel, was dedicated by the Bishop of Bristol on Sunday 23 November 1923. The other change occurred in 1929 when Mr. James and his sister, Mrs. Despard Davies, presented new choir stalls and the organ casing in memory of their mother, Lady James.

New Patron

Not long after his appointment as vicar, Fred Norton raised the matter of the patronage of St. Mary's with the PCC. For some time the trustees had apparently failed to appoint new trustees when one of their number died or retired from the trust, so by 1924 there was only one remaining trustee, Prebendary M.E. Hoets, who lived in Bath. The vicar's concern was, that should anything happen to him, the trust would lapse and the advowson (the right to appoint to a benefice) would be put up for sale and might be acquired by one of the 'party' trusts. It was decided to consult the Bishop and write to Prebendary Hoets, but when a year later it was reported to the PCC that no reply had been received from him and it emerged that he was in very poor health, the vicar was asked to visit him as soon as possible to talk about the future of the patronage. The result was that Prebendary Hoets agreed to transfer the patronage to the Bishop of Bristol with whom it remains. The Order in Council transferring the patronage was dated 13 May 1927.

Another of the matters considered by the PCC in its early days related to the Sunday school that met in the Downleaze area. On the departure of Roger Whytehead, the children who met in his house were accommodated by Mrs. Osborne in her home in Downleaze. But when this was no longer available, the council decided to buy 11 Julian Road. This became known as 'Church House'. It was purchased for £1450, and a further £300 was spent on alterations. Nearly £1000 was quickly raised by subscription towards the cost. The top floors provided a home for the curate, the basement for the caretaker, while the ground floor rooms provided space for the Sunday school and for other committees and organisations. On 29 January 1926 the PCC met there for the first time, and agreed the charges for lettings of Church House: council room - seven shillings and six pence, large room - ten shillings and six pence, the whole floor - one guinea, with a further shilling to be charged if gas for refreshments was required. 'The great gale' of 1928 caused considerable damage to the roof of Church House and although it was repaired it became apparent that a new roof was needed. This cost was £200. Another heavy bill for repairs in 1931 was met by the contributions of the ladies' working party.

Church Finances

The church accounts for 1926 (Appendix 6) reveal a number of interesting items. In common with most churches at this time St. Mary's relied for a considerable portion of its income on pew rents. The difficulty caused by this arrangement was that it was not always known to visitors to the church which particular pews could not be occupied because they were reserved for those who had rented them. In 1929 it was decided to display a plan of "the occupied and unoccupied seats". Another problem was that the family who rented a pew did not always attend services, so that a number of seats were often empty in the centre of the church, with many of the people who were present forced to sit in the side aisles. In 1934, in an attempt to overcome this, it was decided to inform seat holders that, if they were not present when the bell stopped and the organ started playing, their pews would be free for others to occupy.

At St. Mary's, between the two wars, some adult members of the choir received pay and a figure of eight pounds and two shillings in the accounts of 1926 reveal that there were occasions when they seem to have required taxis to get to the services in time. There were those who felt a paid choir was an unnecessary expense, but when the matter was raised in the PCC in January 1924, it was felt that a small number of professional singers were required if the standard of music in the services was to be maintained. The benefit of having a small nucleus of professional singers, who could be relied on to be there at all services, was obviously understood by some others in the congregation because in 1926 voluntary contributions to the choir fund amounted to £54.

Missionary societies were supported with special collections, but the total given to all of them was only just over £59 in 1926. The poor parishes of Bristol and St. Thomas, Eastville, with which Stoke Bishop had historic links, received nearly £64. There is no mention in the accounts of the diocesan quota, which appears to have been dependant on separate gifts to a special fund. We do know however that in 1928 £130 was sent to the diocesan board of finance, while in 1932 the fund only received £90. The vicar went to explain to the bishop that this was due to the loss of number of wealthy supporters of St. Mary's. Rather surprisingly the bishop accepted this explanation and said that there was no need to have a special collection for the quota.

The deficit in the annual accounts for 1926 led the finance committee to consider the level of giving in St. Mary's. They found that the totals for pew rents, collections and the choir fund were stable, but subscriptions to the clergy fund had fallen slightly from £287 in the previous year to £232 in 1926. They suggested to the PCC that an envelope scheme for free will offerings be introduced. The new scheme initially met with some opposition because people wished to be able to give to their favoured funds, but it was retained for 1928 with the vicar writing a letter in the parish magazine explaining why it should be supported. It seems to have had the desired effect because by 1932 the free will offerings were £410 for that year, equalling the amount raised by pew rents and choir fund put together.

Goings and Comings

Tom Miller retired from the headmastership of Stoke Bishop school in 1923 and he was replaced by J. Hill who had been an assistant teacher at the school since 1911. His links with St. Mary's were close and he later became a churchwarden. Early in 1924 A. Tyler died. Had he lived until Easter he would have been verger at St. Mary's for forty two years. He was succeeded as verger by D. Pratley, who had already been serving as sexton for twenty four years. He eventually retired as verger in 1946.

In 1936 Canon Fred Norton left Stoke Bishop to become vicar of All Saints', Clifton. The PCC recorded its appreciation of the untiring and unselfish devotion with which he had served the church in the parish, the inspiration and leadership which he had given unstintingly and the example of goodness and sincerity which he had shown to his people. The churchwardens and the secretary of the council were to consult with the bishop about a new vicar for the parish in the light of the needs, conditions and traditions of Stoke Bishop. The PCC passed unanimously that "the vicar be not an extreme man in either direction, and be in sympathy with the young people of the parish." Clear and brief, but others might agree that, as requirements, they perhaps do not make very favourable comparison with those that guided the original trustees in their search for the right man to serve as vicar of Stoke Bishop.

CHAPTER FOUR

1936 - 1968

This new chapter in the history of Stoke Bishop church begins with the appointment by Bishop Woodward of Canon Sydney Worters as the new vicar. Sydney Worters had been in the diocese of Bristol for all his ministry and, as vicar of Oldland, and then for fourteen years of St. Luke's, Brislington, he had considerable parochial experience before arriving at St. Mary's. He had also been rural dean of Bedminster for eight years. Leslie Williams, who was his curate for a short while at Stoke Bishop, described him as a loving and approachable man, with a lovely sense of humour. He was a simple preacher, and someone who took great care in leading services. He believed in as high a standard as possible for the music of services, for anything less would not be honouring to God. The Bishop wrote, "His experience will be invaluable, and whether of men, of situations or of personal problems, his judgement is at once shrewd and invariably fair." The Bishop thought so highly of him that after the war, while Canon Worters was still vicar of Stoke Bishop, he asked him to be his honorary chaplain. He also told Bishop Cockin, who succeeded him, "When you have consulted all your diocesan officials, and are not satisfied that their advice is sound, go and talk to Worters. I did, and never failed to come away wiser." So for the second time when war came, the parish was in good hands.

One of the concerns of the parochial church council was that the vicar's stipend should be increased and so it decided that as from January 1937 the stipend would be £600, together with a rate free vicarage, the rates at the time being £44. In order to ensure this sum was available, an appeal went out to increase the Endowment Fund. The total raised was £7396 and was very greatly helped by a contribution of £5000 from Miss

Violet Wills. In response to the sum raised by the parish, the Ecclesiastical Commissioners made additional grants to the Endowment Fund over a period of four years. This meant that in 1939 interest on the capital in the Fund contributed £366 towards the stipend, the PCC making up the difference from its own funds. The curate at the time was paid £260 per annum and the verger £105.

Groups for Men and Women

There had been a branch of the Church of England Men's Society in the parish since the beginning of the century, though as far as can be ascertained the numbers attending the meetings were generally small. Now some of the women in the congregation met with Canon Worters, and it was decided to form a Stoke Bishop Church Women's Fellowship, with membership open to any women in the congregation. The first meeting took place with Canon Worters in the chair on 14 April 1937 and by September there were no fewer than 119 members paying a subscription of one shilling and six pence per year. It was to be "an association founded on principle, sustained by devotion, built up by service and warmed by friendship." At their meetings, after prayers, the members formed activity groups - arts and crafts, drama, music, horticulture and support for overseas missions. The music group soon produced a choir which paid visits to old people's homes in other parts of the city, the choir being directed by Sylvia Brenan, with Cecile Barnard playing the piano. Members were also engaged in knitting and making clothes which were distributed to poor children in Bristol. The formation of the women's fellowship in 1937 meant that it was well established by the time of the war, when as a serving group its work became invaluable.

Pew Rents and Finance

From the moment of his arrival in Stoke Bishop, Canon Worters expressed a desire to do away with the system of pew rents. However there were those on the church council who foresaw a considerable drop in the income of the church if they were abolished. It was decided that the vicar should write to all those renting pews telling them of the proposal to abolish pew rents and asking if they would they be willing to commit themselves to financial support for St. Mary's in lieu of the money they were expending in renting a pew. Of the one hundred and five letters sent out, only seven pew holders protested against the proposed change, though thirty five did not reply at all. From the others there came promises of financial support amounting to £290 per annum, which represented a drop in income of £100. In the light of this, by ten votes to five, the parochial church council decided that from Easter Day 1939 all pews would be free. However the pew rent system, even when abolished, continued to make its influence felt because some people still wanted to be able to sit in what they regarded as 'their pew', their family having rented it for years, and resented it if they found somebody else already sitting there. It would be many years before the pews became truly free for all in the mind of every worshipper.

The church accounts for 1939 (appendix 6) reveal a number of interesting details. Prior to the National Health Service, hospitals were always in need of contributions, hence the gift to the Lord Mayor's Hospital Fund, though another gift of eleven shillings and nine pence could not have provided much equipment for the Hospital for Sick Children. The Spanish civil war called forth the gift for the food ship for Spain, while the feared drop in income as a result of the ending of pew rents seems to have been more than made up by freewill offerings and donations. As far as expenditure was concerned, a St. Mary's church treasurer at the end of the twentieth century would look with astonished eyes at an annual heating bill of £39, £18 for printing and stationary and only £37 for the insurance of the church, while the diocesan quota for that year amounted to just £100. In 1939 money was needed for some unexpected work on the church roof and to the organ, as well as to a bulging wall in the churchyard. A special appeal was made and the £1350 needed was raised in four months.

World War II

The air raid sirens sounded in the parish just a few minutes after the Prime Minister had told the country that we were at war with Germany. It was a false alarm and for months the country experienced what has been called the 'phoney war'. Nevertheless during this period important changes were made to the pattern of services in St. Mary's. Dr. Robin Brocklehurst, the churchwarden, reported that the cost of black-out for the church building would be prohibitive and so the early morning communion service moved from 8 a.m. to 8.45 a.m. Later it was restored to 8 a.m. with candles on the communion table giving light for the celebrant and the congregation encouraged to bring small hand torches if they needed to read a prayer book. The evening service in winter was held at 3.30 p.m. Short mid-week war intercessions were held and there was daily prayer for those from the parish on active service. Another change related to the choir. Prior to the war the choir consisted of two professional quartets, but the choir now became voluntary. However Miss M. Stephens, Miss E.K. Bannister, Miss H. Ferribee, Mrs. Nancy Jones and her sister Mrs. E. Williams, and Mr W. Burns continued to sing in the choir and each gave between twenty five and forty years service to St. Mary's as choir members.

In April 1941 a special service was held in church for members of the Home Guard. The danger to the church building from incendiary bombs was recognised and every night when there was an air raid, the staff and students from Clifton Theological College at Stoke House came over to fire watch. This was during term time. During their holidays volunteers were recruited from the parish. Ladders and duck boards gave them access to the roof. There is no record of their ever having to use their stirrup pumps to put out a fire caused by a bomb landing on the roof of the church, but they were always ready and in December 1944 a special service was held for all those who had shared in fire watch duty on the occasion of their 'stand easy'.

Air Raid Damage

The parish as a whole certainly did not escape from the effects of air raids and a first aid post was set up in the village hall to deal with casualties. Bomb damage was caused to 17 Druid Stoke Avenue and to Stoke House, while a bomb that fell on 10 Old Sneed Avenue was probably the one that blew out the clerestory windows and those in the south aisle of the church. When these were restored after the war the opportunity was taken to surround the figures with plain glass which lightened the church considerably. Damage to Church House in Julian Road required a loan from the diocese of £275 while war damage claims were awaited. A whole batch of bombs fell two by two in Sneyd Park, faithfully mirroring the twin bomb racks of a Heinkel III, the pattern suggesting that they were released at a relatively low level. Many of them fell on soft ground and failed to explode. Other places hit included Nazareth House and two houses in Kewstoke Road. An incendiary bomb fell at 21 Ormerod Road.

By far the most damaging incendiary bombs were those that destroyed Stoke Bishop school during the night of 2 December 1940. The immediate requirement was to find alternative accommodation for the children, and this was secured in the short term by places being found at Westbury Park school, but by June the following year the children returned to the Kewstoke Road site with the infants in the school house, which had escaped the effects of the air raid with only minor damage, and the juniors being taught in temporary huts in the school grounds. In due course these huts were inadequate for the numbers of children who required to be taught, so in 1944 the school managers, supported by the education authorities, requested the use of the village hall. Consent had to be delayed because the Ministry of Food was using the hall for the issue of ration books, much to the annoyance of the vicar who felt strongly that the needs of the children should have taken precedence. However, by the autumn term, the hall, with four new gas radiators and with alterations and redecoration paid for by the education authority, accommodated the school during the day time. The regular income from this letting was certainly of great help to the village hall committee.

Another result of the destruction of the school buildings was that the Sunday schools that had met there were replaced by a children's service in church, but in 1944 Sylvia Brenan took pity on the infant children and started a small infant class in a house in Glen Drive. When the numbers outgrew the living room, it moved in 1944 into one of the school huts in Kewstoke Road.

Wartime Ministry

The war drew many people to the church. There were 466 communicants on Easter Day in 1940 and, for a national call to prayer on 3 September 1942, there were nine services in St. Mary's to which it is recorded some 2000 people came. The services included one for two hundred and fifty members of the Home Guard, who were joined by members of the other Civil Defence services. They were not summoned by bells, for the ringing of these was reserved as a warning of invasion, though on 18 November 1942 they were permitted to be rung in celebration of the victory at El Alamein. In spite of the numbers who came to church on special occasions, there was still a concern that St. Mary's should be more effective in its outreach. With this in mind the Reverend P.G. Reddick, later to become archdeacon of Bristol, was invited to speak on the subject of parochial evangelism. Following his talk, a sub-committee was appointed to come forward with suggestions for implementation by the church council. In July 1943 they made the following recommendations,

(1) that prayer should be offered regularly for different areas and sectors of the parish
(2) that a family service with sermon be introduced
(3) that the women's fellowship and the men's society include the subject of evangelism at one of their meetings
(4) that street representatives be appointed to report needs to the clergy
(5) that cards be placed in all the pews for newcomers.

It is interesting to note that while few of these recommendations were acted on immediately, it was not very long before most were adopted as important aspects of the outreach of the parish church. Street representatives were appointed in 1944. They were told to act as newsgatherers for the clergy, but to avoid being busybodies. Cards for newcomers to fill in, if they wished the clergy to call, appeared in the pews about the same time.

As early as 1936 the church council had wondered whether Church House in Julian Road was serving a worthwhile purpose, and had considered selling it. The same idea re-emerged in 1940 when a purchaser was found and a sale was all but agreed for £700. However opposition to the sale was so strong that Sydney Worters had to ask the purchaser to rescind the sale, which he very kindly agreed to do. This meant that Church House was available in 1943 to be used as a 'services canteen'.

The number of servicemen and women in and around Bristol had been building up in readiness for the D Day landings in France and so there was a need for somewhere for those camped and billeted in the area to come for their breaks. The catering management was in the hands of Mrs. Brocklehurst and with sixty volunteer helpers the canteen was open from 10-11 a.m. on Monday, Wednesday and Friday, daily from 1-2 p.m. and each evening from 7.30-9.30 p.m. In the first nine months 58495 hot drinks and 1008 cold drinks were served and 28170 meals. This marvellous piece of war service drew letters of appreciation from the commanding officers of the troops who came in such numbers to the friendly and welcoming atmosphere of Church House.

During these war years the appearance of the environs of St. Mary's changed. The church railings together with those around some of the graves were removed to help the war effort. In the church council there seems to have been a long discussion about whether the yew trees near the church would have to be felled or whether it would be adequate for them to be trimmed. However it was discovered that the tree roots were growing under the walls of the tower, so they had to be felled. Inside the building, a grand piano, the gift of Mr. and Mrs. Vincent Barnard, was a most useful addition to the church furniture. On the night of 18 January 1945 a gale blew down two stone crosses, one from above the James chapel, which half buried itself in the grass below, the other from the west end, which in its fall smashed many tiles on the nave and aisle roofs, brought down a large piece of guttering and scattered its fragments as far as the lych-gate.

There was joy on 23 April 1945 when the black-out ended and the lights in the church could shine out again. In the following month came the retirement of D. Pratley. He had served St. Mary's for forty-six years as sexton, and, during the last twenty-one of those years, as verger. When in the summer of 1945 the war in Europe came to an end, it was decided that the collections in church on the following Sunday should be given for the needs of the Christian Churches in Europe. In due course thirty-nine names would be added to the Stoke Bishop War Memorial.

Discovering Needs

In 1948 St. Mary's undertook a parochial survey. A letter and questionnaire was sent to every home in the parish and this was followed up with a personal visit. One thousand two hundred replies were received and five hundred and thirty three of them stated that they attended St. Mary's. The effort involved in the survey was not wasted. The vicar reported that he noted "a quickening of the spiritual life of the parish with a heartening increase in the congregation." Six committees of the church council were set up to deal with different aspects of the replies relating to church services and church activities, youth and children, visiting and social activities. Arising from their deliberations a number of important changes took place.

In September 1948 a weekly family service from 10 - 10.35 a.m. was introduced into the Sunday programme of services and, although only three families came to the first service, the numbers quickly increased to around twelve families who came regularly. Canon Worters probably felt it was not quite his scene, so the principal of Clifton theological college, the Reverend John Cobb was invited to take it and later services were also taken by the Reverend Fred Barff who had retired to live in the parish.

At the same time a renewed effort was made to recruit and train more Sunday school teachers. It was decided to form a bible study group and prayer group. It started in the home of Edith Laxton and later moved to the home of Bill and Mary Burkett. A new effort also was made to see that every road in the parish had a representative, while area reps were chosen whose responsibility it was to pass information on to the clergy. As a result of the findings of the social committee, the annual Patronal Festival garden party started and was held in the gardens of Heatherdale in Mariners Drive. It was estimated that between five and six hundred people attended this in 1948. Another social occasion was the parish breakfast which followed the early communion service. Sausages, bacon and lots else, all cooked, so we are told, "on an awful old cooker in Church House."

It would seem that, having led the church into making a number of important new initiatives, Sydney Worters felt that it was time for him to move on, stating in the parish magazine that the task required to be in the hands of a younger man. In 1949 he accepted the invitation to become rector of Winterbourne and was succeeded by Canon Henry Louis

Bothamley. He had been vicar of Clifton Parish Church and had seen his church building there completely destroyed by enemy bombs during the war.

Schools

In Stoke Bishop it was the school that was destroyed. It had been a church school, but after the war when a new school had to be built, there was no way the church could face the capital expenditure required for a new building. The school managers were told by the Ministry of Education that the site for the proposed school would be at Cedar Park. A special meeting of parishioners was held on 7 December 1948 and as a result the managers decided that the only course open to them was to make the school a voluntarily controlled school under the Local Education Authority. It meant that the constitution of the management committee was changed to two foundation managers, one of whom had to be the principal officiating minister, the other appointed by the Bristol Diocesan Education Authority and four representatives appointed by the Local Authority.

Cedar Park school was officially opened by the Minister of Education, George Tomlinson, on 13 April 1951, and six days later the Bishop of Bristol came and dedicated the school. But so pressed were the authorities for room that six classes had started to use some of the accommodation in the previous November. It was the first voluntarily controlled Church of England primary school opened under the Bristol Education Authority. The school was planned for two hundred pupils, but from the outset it exceeded that number, and for some time the Kewstoke Road building and huts continued to be used.

Prior to the war, and for some while afterwards, the parish also attracted a number of private schools. Before the theological college moved in to Stoke House, there had been a girls' school there, closing down in 1931. There was also Hampton House school for girls in Hazelwood Road, St. Goars boys' prep school at the Mythe in Julian Road, and another school for boys, St. David's, in Ivywell Road. Colwyn school for girls was where the Ridgewood flats now stand. Boys and girls attended Sneyd Park prep school which stood in Old Sneed Avenue, while

Sydney Worters
1936-1949

Henry Bothamley
1949-1954

Norman Hulbert
1955-1960

Photograph taken in 1960, St Mary's Centenary year
From Left to Right: *Professor Robin Brocklehurst (who was vicar's warden during the war and served for a total of 21 years), Canon Bothamley (former vicar), Prebendary Treen, Rev.Oliver Tompkins, (Bishop of Bristol), Canon Hulbert (vicar), Rev.W. Parmer (from India), Tom Barr (people's warden).*

Avondale, another boys' prep school, occupied Braidlea House. When this school closed in the 1970's the headmaster asked if the school war memorial could be kept by the church. It is on the wall leading from the church to the Church Rooms. Another prep school for boys was called XIV and survived until the 1980's. The buildings now house a residential nursing home. Today the number of nursing homes exceeds the earlier private schools in the parish.

Sunday Schools

It is interesting to note the pattern of Sunday worship at St. Mary's that Canon Bothamley inherited. Holy Communion was celebrated each Sunday at 8 a.m. and on the first Sunday in the month at 12 noon. The other services were a Family Service from 10-10.35 a.m., followed by Morning Prayer at 11 a.m. At 3 p.m. there was a senior children's service in church normally taken by the curate, and the other Sunday schools took place at the same time. Evening Prayer was at 6.30 p.m. The need for Sunday schools had emerged from the parochial survey responses. Trying to teach large numbers of children of a wide age range in the church was proving an impossible task. So the children's sub-committee of the church council felt that it would be right to re-start the Sunday schools on a large scale. They invited Miss Wright, the diocesan organiser to come to the parish and give a series of lectures on new methods in teaching and at the end of the course a number of those who attended offered themselves as Sunday school teachers.

1949 saw the beginning of the new Sunday schools, scattered across the parish. In the temporary huts on Kewstoke Road that housed Stoke Bishop school, the kindergarten was joined by a junior department and numbers increased rapidly. The question of opening elsewhere was considered and in 1950 Mr. and Mrs. Eyre-Brook offered their home, Druids Mead, which was close to the fast developing Cedar Park estate. In the same year a room in Church House accommodated an infant department. Soon the numbers in these Sunday schools was over 130. Then with the opening of the new school in Cedar Park, the infant department, now too numerous for a private house, moved into the new school buildings, together with a new junior department. By 1952 there were 320 children in the Sunday schools and once a month they all met together for a service in St. Mary's. But as can be imagined in order to staff these there was a constant call for more teachers, as well as pianists.

Service Overseas

St. Mary's had always supported the Church Missionary Society, and now one of its parishioners, Dr. Arthur Laxton, was to go abroad as a missionary with the Society. He went initially to serve in a hospital in Cairo, but then moved to the CMS hospital at Lui in Southern Sudan. A quite different form of service was given by a communicant member of St. Mary's who went out to Korea in 1954. Lieutenant Terence Waters was seriously wounded in the battle of the Imjin river, was taken prisoner and died. He was posthumously awarded the George Cross and the citation read, "He was a young inexperienced officer ... yet he set an example of the highest gallantry." Another fatality, recorded in the roll of honour, was Sergeant Mervyn Paice, murdered by Jewish terrorists during the British occupation of Palestine in 1947.

The Missing Hall

For a long time it had been clear that the work of the church was hampered by the lack of a hall. As long ago as 1946 a triangular plot of land on the north side of the church had been purchased and in November 1950 the church council was told that the owner of Huntworth on the south side was prepared to sell approximately a third of the grounds for £1000, though the restrictive covenants prevented the building of anything other than houses and coach houses on the land. Despite this, the decision was made to purchase the land and the damaged stables were rebuilt with the help of a grant from the War Damage Commissioners as a verger's cottage. In 1951 Dame Violet Wills gave a plot of land in Church Road as a site for a new vicarage, but four years later this land was sold, with the consent of the donor, and the capital used to augment the stipend of the incumbent. In 1952 a church hall building fund was started and in 1954 an extra piece of land with frontage on Mariner's Drive was bought. All this meant that the church now owned land to the north and south of the church.

It was at this point that Canon Bothamley announced to the parish that he had accepted the invitation to become the vicar of the parish of St. Mary Magdalene, Taunton. St. Mary's, with its magnificent tower, was the parish church of the county town, so his work would be to draw together the church and the civic life of Taunton. During the five years he was vicar of Stoke Bishop, his foresight and leadership enabled St. Mary's to acquire the land around the church. His encouragement led to the growth of the family service and he saw greatly increased numbers of children attending Sunday schools. It was in his time that the baptismal roll fellowship started for the mothers of the babies who had been baptised in St. Mary's, which in 1952 became the young wives group with a much wider membership. Outside the parish he was the rural dean of Clifton (Stoke Bishop was in the Clifton deanery in those days) and he was elected a proctor in Convocation. In the James chapel he left us the delightful stained glass window of St. Chad in memory of his parents and his love of the parish was reflected in his retiring to live at the Cromlech, on Druid Hill. He was married after he left Stoke Bishop, so with his young wife and family he worshipped again in St. Mary's until his death.

His successor was another who came to Stoke Bishop from St. Luke's, Brislington. Canon Mike Hulbert was collated and inducted at a service in St. Mary's on 11 February 1955. In July that year the church council decided to bring matters to a head by applying to the appropriate authority for permission to build a church hall on the land to the south of the church. A year later the city authorities gave permission for a hall and car park, but, when application was made to the lands tribunal for the removal of the restrictive covenants, this was refused. The proceedings are said to have cost £300, which included the costs of the eleven objectors. Other plans were then discussed. These included the purchase of a house named St. Mary's on Stoke Hill, or to use the site of the old school on Kewstoke Road. However the first was found to be impossible to convert for parish purposes and there was impossibly poor access to the old school site for cars.

Contact with Parishioners

One of the features of the ministry of Canon Hulbert was his desire to meet the people of the parish. Canon and Mrs. Hulbert held a succession of coffee parties at the vicarage for residents in every street. There were thirty of these parties with a total attendance of about eight hundred. Mrs. Hulbert also started a branch of the Mothers' Union, and at the first gathering in March 1956 there were twelve present, eight of whom had been members in other parishes before coming to Stoke Bishop. This meant that there were now three women's groups connected with St. Mary's: women's fellowship, young wives' fellowship and Mothers' Union.

Canon Hulbert discussed with the parochial church council the introduction of a choral celebration of holy communion for the first Sunday of each month. This was agreed, but in the parish magazine he wrote, "I want to dispel any fears that this is the first step towards making us a 'high church'." The choral setting was that of Merbecke, and after congregational singing practices, the service began in February 1957 with 130 people receiving communion and the vicar reporting that the service was sung very beautifully. That same year St. Mary's responded to an invitation from the Congregational church in Sneyd Park to a monthly joint bible study. The leaders were alternately clergy from each church, but it provided an opportunity through discussion of the bible passages to get to know the members of this other church in the parish.

Links with Lawrence Weston

Opportunity also arose for people from St. Mary's to engage in Christian service outside the parish. In the newly developed housing estate of Lawrence Weston, the vicar was trying to visit the homes, and asked for help. A band of men under the leadership of George Sisman and Frank Evans undertook this and it led on to an increasing involvement of Stoke Bishop people in giving their skills, money and time to helping the tiny group of church people there. Marjorie Gillespie mobilised a women's working party and jumble was delivered for sales in Lawrence Weston on many occasions. Partly through these links with St. Peter's in Lawrence Weston, when the Bishop issued his appeal for new church building, St. Mary's exceeded the amount asked of it by several hundred pounds. Because the consecration of the new church building in Lawrence Weston coincided with the centenary of St. Mary's, it was agreed that the first

£1500 of the centenary appeal would be given to St. Peter's, and this money provided an organ for their church.

St. Mary's Centenary

As the centenary year approached it was felt that another effort must be made to solve the problem of the lack of a church hall. A committee put forward the suggestion that a modern vicarage be built on land close to the church and that the 'old' vicarage be converted into a flat for a married curate and for use as committee rooms, while adjoining the house a one-story hall should be built in the garden. The amount required for this would be £25000, and the appeal was launched in February 1960. The vicar planned to sit in church on 13 February to receive gifts, but a few days before he was struck down by a heart attack. Churchwardens and sidesmen deputised for him.

One of those churchwardens, Robin Brocklehurst, announced that he would have to resign at the next vestry meeting. The bishop had asked him to take on the chairmanship of what was to be a most important committee dealing with Christian stewardship in the diocese. He had been vicar's warden for twenty-one years serving under three vicars, during which time his unfailing regularity at services and his immense knowledge of the church were matched by his self-effacing sincerity. Whenever a job needed doing, whether it was collecting waste paper for sale, making cakes, or lending a large house for a party, Mrs. Brocklehurst was always there. As husband and wife they both did an immense amount for St. Mary's.

The centenary services took place on Sunday 13 March. The vicar was able to be there, though looking far from well. Canon Bothamley preached at the family service and the Bishop of Bristol at the special centenary thanksgiving service at 11 a.m. The preacher at evensong was Canon L.S. Alford, the son of Canon Alford who had been vicar of Stoke Bishop before the first world war.

In connection with the centenary, the vicar had invited the Principal of Wycliffe Hall, Oxford, with twenty ordinands to spend a week of work and worship in the parish, during Holy Week. Each morning was spent in corporate study of the passion of Christ. In the afternoon the team became a working party undertaking manual work in the parish, sawing wood for one elderly parishioner, gardening for another, visiting and taking out people from the blind home in Downleaze, scraping down the woodwork of the lych gate, and clearing the weeds from the churchyard. Each evening the addresses of the Reverend F.J. Taylor, later to become Bishop of Sheffield, brought the events of Holy Week to light in a way that was rewarding for all who were there.

Mike Hulbert died on 20 April 1960. The last weeks of his life were clouded by anxiety over the result of the appeal which at first was disappointing, and worry about the strong opposition of his neighbours to the idea of a hall in the grounds of the vicarage. But he left behind a parish mourning the loss of a much loved vicar. In outlook he was tolerant, with a keen sense of humour and a wide experience of human nature and of the work of a pastor. He and Helen, his wife, made people feel perfectly at ease with their warm friendliness, and the vicarage was most truly an 'open house'. Of Mike Hulbert a member of the congregation wrote after his death, "He possessed the inspiring humility of a good man, in whom one could place absolute trust and confidence".

New Vicar and New Buildings

The parish did not have long to wait before the name of its new vicar was known. It was to be Canon Leslie Williams, who for a short time had been a curate at St. Mary's and was at the time vicar of St. Michael and All Angels, Bishopston. The announcement was made in June, but his collation and institution did not take place until 7 October 1960. Prebendary H.M. Treen, a retired priest living in Clifton, was appointed priest-in-charge for the period when there was no vicar. Mrs. Hulbert moved to a flat in Clifton, and, though she had been out of the profession for thirty years, bravely went back to teaching.

At the Parochial Church Council meeting on 28 October it was agreed that the building of a new vicarage should commence as soon as possible, and in fact a year later the Williams family were able to move in to the newly constructed house, which was blessed by the Bishop of Malmesbury on 18 November. It had cost £10527. Leslie Williams told a parishioner that in diocesan circles it was considered the model vicarage.

"And do they look on you as the model vicar?" he was asked. After a moment's thought, perhaps remembering his brushes with authority, he gravely expressed "considerable doubts."

But what was to happen to the old vicarage on Stoke Hill? The plan to build a hall in the grounds had met with considerable opposition and so a parish meeting was arranged in the village hall on 28 November 1960, and all objectors were expressly invited to attend. The meeting attracted a large attendance and the vicar, after explaining the church's need for a hall requested that those present should speak their minds, promising that no offence would be taken. A number of objectors spoke against the proposed hall, and the vicar closed a long and good humoured meeting by promising that the church council would consider all the points raised. But during the meeting Mr. Pritchard, the secretary of the village hall trustees, took everyone by surprise by proposing that the church should take over the village hall. Seventy five years earlier St. Mary's and its members had been the prime movers in getting the hall built, but it was entrusted to a body of trustees, of whom the incumbent would always be one, to be held by them for the use of those living in the parish. The site was owned by the city and county of Bristol who granted a lease to the trustees for a peppercorn rent.

A number of meetings were held of the relevant bodies and by May 1962 the village hall trustees had agreed to surrender their lease.The city had offered a 21 year lease, with an option to renew for a further 21 years, which the church council was ready to accept. In the light of this the old vicarage was sold by auction for £7735 to become the site for Eastmead Court. The charity commissioners had to give their approval of the transfer of the hall to the church, so there was a further long delay until, in March 1964, all seemed ready for the takeover. But then the diocese stepped in. They refused permission for St. Mary's to enter into the lease. No one, it appears, had thought of seeking approval of the diocese at an earlier stage because it was assumed that they would agree to something the parish needed so much. One can imagine how very frustrating the decision of the diocese must have been for all who had been involved in these long negotiations. However with benefit of hindsight, it can be seen that St. Mary's was saved from what would have been a considerable expense in maintaining this old building, a building which

Leslie Williams chairs a PCC meeting
With him (left to right) *are John Dodd who served for 41 years as PCC secretary and Frank Evans, churchwarden*

Morning service in 1962. The controversial screen was erected in 1904 and removed in 1966

they would never own and over which, because of the original trust deed, they would never have had complete control. In any case, thanks to the impatience of the vicar, another and superior plan was already in hand.

As early as May 1961 Canon Williams had tentatively suggested to the PCC that an extension might be built on the north side of the church to include a new choir vestry, committee rooms and a large room in which the Sunday school could meet. By June he had secured in writing the removal of the restrictive covenants on the land. A year later the church council paid a visit to Hanham to inspect a new hall built by Messrs. F.H. Elbrow Ltd. who had built the vicarage and, after delays in obtaining planning permission, this firm began work on the site in November 1963. In anticipation of its completion Church House in Julian Road was sold for £4850.

The foundation stone of the new building was laid by a 'team of old residents', Sylvia Brenan and Cecile Barnard, both of whom had been born in the parish, and Professor Robin Brocklehurst. When it became known that the village hall would not be managed by the church, assurance had to be given to the immediate neighbours that the new rooms would not be licensed for music and dancing, nor would they be available for general letting. The Church Rooms were dedicated by the Bishop of Bristol on 1 October 1964. Mrs Hulbert was present to open the Hulbert Room in memory of her husband. The aim of the centenary appeal had been achieved, though Horace Pullen, the appeal treasurer had some years of work to do before all the money was raised. St. Mary's was greatly indebted to Francis Hannam, the architect of the vicarage, who gave his skills for the Church Rooms in an honorary capacity, while the technical and practical experience of Bill Goodwin, chairman of the buildings committee, was invaluable. But there is no doubt that without the drive and enthusiasm of Leslie Williams, overcoming many irritations, difficulties and frustrations, the dream might never have come true.

'Meet the Church'

St. Mary's was not solely concerned about the extension of its buildings. A small committee met in the vicarage to study ways and means of making the witness of the church more effective in the parish. With the post-war housing developments, the population of the parish according to the 1961 census was now 4856, double the population in 1931. The committee came up with the idea of a 'Meet the Church Week'. This took place during a week in October 1962, ironically in the village hall. Prior to the week a large body of men from the congregation visited homes in the parish to issue invitations and the village hall was made ready for the exhibition of photographs depicting aspects of the life of the church and its organisations. These photographs and the brochure for the week were the work of Ronald Warne, who did so much to make the exhibition memorable and attractive. A number of firms offered their help. The exhibition was planned by Mr. Farrow, of Ford, Farrow and Partners, advertising consultants, while Lewis's of Broadmead loaned and erected all the hardboard panels and supports and E.S & A Robinson provided envelopes and other material.

On each morning of the week from 9.30-10.30 a.m. children from the various schools in the parish visited the exhibition and were shown a film. Area representatives held coffee mornings for those from their area and there were tea parties in the afternoon when different organisations acted as hosts. The village hall was filled each evening for talks given by a very distinguished team of speakers, the Bishops of Blackburn and Bristol, the Provost of Birmingham and the Dean of Bristol and the Reverend Eric James, who was then the vicar of Camberwell. Regular members of the congregation were asked to stay away from these talks to allow space for others. It is impossible to assess the results of 'Meet the Church Week', but certainly many people learnt what the Church stood for and in particular what St. Mary's was like and what it was doing. Over 1000 people attended the exhibition during the week.

Links with Other Churches

Around this time the ecumenical movement began to affect the thinking of the churches of the area. At the end of 1961 a ministers' fraternal was established for the vicars and curates of Stoke Bishop and Westbury Parish Churches, and the ministers of Sneyd Park Congregational, Westbury Methodist and Westbury Baptist Churches. Sadly on 11 May

1962, Sneyd Park Congregational Church held its closing service because the members felt it was no longer right for so small a group to continue in so large a building. On 14 June the inaugural service of the Westbury Council of Christian Churches was held for the four remaining churches, and the first representatives on the council from St. Mary's were Judith Atkinson and Ralph Vincent. A year later Monsignor Joe Buckley, of the Sacred Heart Roman Catholic Church in Henleaze, had joined the ministers' fraternal, and later the Sacred Heart Church became part of the Westbury Council of Christian Churches, but were required by the rules of their church to have observer status rather than full membership.

The council arranged lectures, study groups, and organised services for the week of prayer for Christian unity, including the exchange of pulpits. In 1965 it joined with the Henleaze churches in a survey which involved visiting every home in the entire Westbury, Henleaze and Stoke Bishop area. A vast amount of information was recorded, though how much use was made of it is open to some doubt and in a society that was becoming increasingly mobile, much of information quickly became out of date. But one result of the survey was the establishment of an ecumenically organised road warden scheme. This was an imaginative conception, but both because of the size of the area, and all the different churches involved, it became difficult to administer successfully. It also had the sad effect of creating some confusion for the already existing road representatives of St. Mary's. However the co-operation of the churches of the Westbury Council of Churches worked wonderfully well in arranging an annual Christmas shopping expedition for the disabled from many parts of the city. Large numbers of cars set out for Woolworths in Broadmead for a special after hours opening and this continued for many years until the character of the store changed, making it less useful for the shoppers.

Important Changes

A letter appeared in the parish magazine for July 1964 from Mr. Arthur Eyre-Brook. "I have worshipped in St. Mary's for 18 years," he wrote, "but time has not mellowed my antipathy for the wrought iron screen, beautiful though it may be in itself. The architect has designed and succeeded in producing a very beautiful House of God, with elegant line and pleasing proportions. These seem to me to have been ruined in any view from the nave by the addition of the screen." He went on to cite St. Stephen's in the city where the original beauty of the church had been restored by the removal of a similar screen and he hoped that the same move might be considered at St. Mary's. In subsequent issues there were letters for and against the idea, including one from a choirboy, who said choirboys could not concentrate on things throughout every service and he was "frightened that the removal of the screen may give the congregation a clearer view of our activities, which the vicar kindly ignores most of the time."

A spirited discussion on a proposal to remove the screen took place at the annual meeting on 27 March 1966 and a vote was taken at a subsequent special meeting which showed 80 for and 60 against its removal. The PCC then applied for a faculty, but the chancellor of the diocese intervened and said that he would decide the issue at a consistory court. This took place in the Church Rooms on 19 November. The case for removal was made by Mrs. Brenan, while Mr. Ryman spoke up in defence of the screen. The verdict of the chancellor was to grant a faculty for the screen to be taken down, while to the relief of the church the costs of the court and legal fees were all waived. The delay caused by the consistory court meant the removal could not coincide with the major decoration of the church. This included the brightly painted rafters in the choir and the introduction of a new lighting scheme. It was planned for September 1966 and cost around £3000. The church was shut for a month, with all services in the Church Rooms, while weddings were conducted in the chapel of Wills Hall.

The 1960s were to see a number of other changes. With the opening of the Church Rooms, the Sunday schools which met at different venues at 3 p.m. were now brought together at the advertised time of 10.20 a.m. The children were encouraged to come with their parents to the first part of the 10 a.m. Family Service, leaving for the Church Rooms at the time of the sermon. The numbers of children attending the afternoon schools had dropped considerably from the high figures of the early 1950's, but there were still those who sent their children to Sunday school in order to enjoy a peaceful afternoon themselves. Now with the change of time, and this link with the Family Service, it meant that fewer children whose parents did not come to church attended Sunday school, but on the other hand there is no doubt that some parents were introduced to church by coming with their children to the Family Service.

In 1967 the Parochial Church Council decided not to replace the worn quarter hammers of the church clock and to leave the church clock striking the hour only, but a year later the whole striking mechanism was abandoned. Also in 1967 the arrival of a married curate with two daughters, the Reverend Nicholas Monk, necessitated the purchase of 7 Little Stoke Road, which was to remain the home of successive curates.

Leslie Williams was installed as archdeacon of Bristol in the cathedral on 29 July 1967, though he remained vicar of Stoke Bishop until the end of the year, when he moved into a new archdeacon's residence at 29 Old Sneed Avenue. As vicar of St. Mary's he brought to the task the energy and dynamic leadership which led to the building of the Church Rooms and the successful 'Meet the Church Week'. David Sansum, before becoming curate of Stoke Bishop, enquired of a colleague who had served under Leslie Williams in another parish, just what his future boss was going to be like. "His bark is worse than his bite," he was told, "In fact he barks a great deal, but hardly ever bites." David Sansum on leaving Stoke Bishop after four years said, "I cannot improve on this assessment. But under his outspoken manner there lies, I discovered, an essential kindliness and a very deep devotion." Known affectionately as Law on account of his initials, he had achieved much in his seven years as vicar.

CHAPTER FIVE

(by Keith Sheather)

1968 - 1992

After a short four week interregnum overseen by the curate, Nicholas Monk, the new vicar, the Reverend Alastair Roy Henderson, was collated and inducted on Friday 26 January by the Bishop of Malmesbury and Archdeacon of Bristol. At 41, Roy Henderson, as he preferred to be called, was the youngest vicar so far appointed to St Mary's. He had three children, the youngest only a few months old. "As the possessor of a young family, I am naturally delighted to find we have a Family Service at St Mary's. In some churches children are still regarded as an annoying nuisance to worshippers." Throughout his ministry he never lost his love for children and that ministry was to be a long one, taking him from father to grandfather. When he left Stoke Bishop in 1992, it was to retire. During his twenty four years, second only to David Wright's ministry in length, he initiated many changes that were to have a profound effect on the worship and witness of St Mary's.

The Parish

During the seventies and eighties the accelerated growth in population of Stoke Bishop had slowed down. Between 1971 and 1991 the number of people living in the parish rose by only 500. This small increase was largely accounted for by flat building and in-filling. One by one the grand estate houses that dominated large areas of Sneyd Park were pulled down and replaced with flats or town houses. Towerleaze, Goodeve and Marklands rose from the ashes of large

Victorian houses like Towerleaze, the Towers and Oakfield House, while Glenavon Park was built on the lands of Old Sneyd Park. In Stoke Bishop Lodge Court and Howecroft Gardens supplanted Howecroft. For the church the new developments provided opportunity but unexpected difficulties - how to gain access when flats, built in "favour of cubic living", were armed with sophisticated security devices designed to keep the casual visitor out.

As Bristol's financial and hi-tech industries expanded, the pressure on Stoke Bishop to provide housing for incoming professionals intensified. Land prices rose and the temptation for owners to sell off part of their gardens for development became irresistible. The rush to in-fill was by the eighties threatening those leafy qualities that made the parish attractive in the first place. Pressure groups were formed to stem the flow. By the late eighties developers turned their attentions to Stoke Bishop's remaining green field sites. Two playing fields - the Grove and the sports ground adjacent to Cedar Park - fell victim to the bulldozer, but for housing and not, as originally proposed, for supermarkets.

The New Vicar

An appreciation in the magazine at the end of his ministry spoke of "Roy Henderson's consistent and prayerful ministry, his steady and wise hand at the helm." Within months of his arrival in the church these qualities were very much in evidence. At his first PCC meeting he literally put a welcoming face on the proceedings by supporting the decision to adopt the practice at communion whereby the celebrant *faces* the congregation.

Equally the Council were to be in no doubt there would be a firm guiding hand behind their deliberations. "The Council warmly welcomed our new Vicar at its first meeting under his chairmanship. He succeeded, by the exercise of gentle firmness, in bringing the business to an end in two and a quarter hours." This leadership showed, too, in his immediately taking on the editorship of the magazine with the retirement of Joan Gray after nine years. It gave him a powerful voice with which to direct parochial thinking. What he wrote 'from the vicarage' ranged over the widest subjects that were of concern to Christians. His articles, although thought provoking, were always practical in their clear exposition of the way the Christian should react, whether the subject was nuclear disarmament, strikes or the diocesan quota.

There also lurked beneath the surface a strong competitive trait, that for most of the time he kept in check, but emerged on the sports field. At his first Patronal Garden Party he introduced family sports which were to be a regular and well advertised feature of subsequent Summer Days. Winners were always recorded in the magazine. He relaxed on the playing field. He loved cricket and rugby, but played golf as often as he could. On one occasion, playing for Bristol in the annual inter-diocesan competition, he achieved a hole in one, though he and his opponent spent nearly five minutes searching for the ball in the bunkers and rough before thinking to look in the hole.

Changes in Liturgy and Services

One of the first issues confronting the new vicar was communion and the Family Service. On his arrival he found it was being proposed to replace Matins with a Family Communion service in which the children would join their parents at the communion rail to receive blessing. Feelings were strong for and against. Some felt the communion service was "not suitable for children who are too young to receive communion", while others welcomed the opportunity of worshipping as a family at the Lord's Table.

The PCC made the unprecedented move of arranging a weekend away to discuss the matter. They spent Friday night and Saturday at 'Penscot' a small guesthouse in the Mendip village of Shipham, "set amid - and without bias toward - the parish church on the one hand and the village inn on the other hand .... Meeting in this relaxed atmosphere produced some unexpected experiences, including a new relationship with one's fellow councillors." The outcome was a compromise - Family Communion on the fifth Sunday. It wasn't until 1978, ten years later, that it became monthly.

Throughout the seventies the Church of England was struggling to produce a new prayer book. The 1967 service of Holy Communion was introduced in 1968 and used at most communion services to allow people to get used to it. Questionnaires, parish meetings and PCC discussions gave expression to the liveliness of the debate. Typically for St Mary's the first questionnaire was evenly balanced - 51% in favour of the '67 service, 49% for the Book of Common Prayer. A second service (Series III) only confirmed the trend and when the completed Alternative Service Book appeared in 1980 the words in its Preface that it was designed to "supplement the Book of Common Prayer, not to supersede it" seemed to reflect the experience of St Mary's precisely. An elaborate pattern of alternating services appeared that required nimbleness of mind to understand.

The new services were the start of a gradual process of relaxation and informality in worship. The 'passing of the Peace' in the communion service caused some consternation at first. The vicar described it as resulting in "unholy chaos." When confronted with the possibility of shaking one's neighbour's hand there was much apprehension. Were people to introduce themselves? Were they to hug each other? How was the handclasp to be carried out? The vicar finally pronounced: "a normal handshake with the second hand added to it........ We are after all members of a family gathered for a very special meal. The least we can do is to greet one another as if this were true."

Another important change, which dated from the Penscot weekend, was to replace Prayer Book Matins as the basis of the Family Service with a new simplified form of service more suitable for the children who attended the first part. Hymn books with new hymns and new 'modern' words in familiar hymns followed - '100 Hymns for Today' in 1971 and 'Hymns for Today's Church' in 1973 with pew copies of the New English Bible purchased in the same year. Baptisms now took place regularly in the Family Service and the church purchased a moveable font, thereby "restoring to the vicar his salad bowl." The pews around the main font were removed in October 1975 to provide a more adaptable space and allow the congregation to talk to the visiting preacher after the services.

The annual Patronal Garden Party was held in the grounds of Heatherdale, a large house opposite the church
This picture was taken around 1962. When the house was demolished, the Garden Party moved to Stoke Lodge and was renamed Summer Day

10.30 Experiment

When Roy Henderson arrived there were three, sometimes four, morning services. This put pressure on the clergy particularly when the 10 a.m. Family Communion Service over-ran and caused the 11.15 Matins to start late. In 1980 it was proposed to bring the two services together for a combined service starting at 10.30 to foster a "sense of unity and fellowship" and to give the clergy more breathing space. To allow the congregation to get used to the idea, all morning services throughout October were combined and started at 10.30. The experiment, as so often happened at St Mary's, was indecisive and a further trial period was set for March the following year.

These were clearly weeks of heated debate and a note of frustration appeared in the vicar's front page for April when he appealed to people to fill in the second questionnaire, "As you can imagine, there have been times when I have felt nostalgic for the old days when vicars were supreme autocrats, made all the decisions and everybody else was left to like it or lump it." He urged people to "pray that in spite of our differences we may still be eager to work and worship 'in the unity of the Spirit and in the bond of peace'." The questionnaire produced a 59.6% in favour of change, a 10% swing since the previous October. But this fell short of the two thirds majority that the PCC felt could justify permanent change, particularly when the questionnaire revealed that, of those who had previously attended at 11.15, less than half were in favour. The experiment was abandoned. Many were disappointed, not least the vicar. But one change was introduced later that made the clergy's life easier. In May 1984 the 10 a.m. Family Service was brought forward by fifteen minutes "to enable the clergy to join others for coffee in the Church Rooms."

House Churches

A cryptic note appeared in the PCC notes in August 1969 requesting "the vicar and Pastoral Committee to inaugurate 'house churches' in the autumn of 1970 or earlier." It was the first intimation of a structure that was to have a profound effect on the life of St Mary's. On 26 October the vicar preached a sermon that began to prepare the congregation for the revolution ahead. There were very real fears that the proposed house churches would have a detrimental effect on the corporate life of the church.

A series of questions appeared in the magazine. There was concern that house churches would reduce the numbers going to church. If lay people led them, as proposed, was it not a question of the blind leading the blind? Were they not just going to be groups of "holy huddles." Roy Henderson sought to allay fears by showing what the church was like in the New Testament. "The Church met in houses. ……. Every Christian was involved in the life and work of the church. There were no professional, full-time clergymen." In the same way the new house churches would not be mere discussion groups but would embrace all activities of the church, "worship, fellowship, study and encouragement in the faith, the service of others and evangelism. ….. Real problems and issues can be thought out in the fellowship of other Christians and we can learn from one another."

Further articles and a number of coffee evenings prepared the way and on Sunday 11 October the Bishop of Bristol, Oliver Tomkins, commissioned St Mary's first house church leaders at a special Family Service. In his sermon the Bishop spoke of how the house church "will enable us to cultivate personal relationships...... build up mature and equipped Christians……. (become) a bridge into a world which does not care about the church."

Despite the early suspicions the house churches flourished. One year on eight people testified in the magazine to benefits they had gained in belonging to one. Fifteen years later the vicar could write encouragingly of thirteen house churches that had grown from the original five. On average 200 people were attending them each month. In 1986 the name changed to house group to avoid confusion with the evangelical House Church movement set up by a group of Christians who had broken away from existing denominations and were meeting in each other's houses. As time went on problems arose. Some groups grew too large and had to make the painful decision to divide. Others ossified as the members grew old together. Yet overall the house groups had a great effect on the spiritual growth of the church.

The Church Family

As the PCC had their weekend away, so the congregation as a whole had the chance to spend a weekend together away from the parish. At a PCC meeting in March 1970 it was reported that "young people have proposed a 'Parish House Party' at some delectable place later in the year." That "delectable" place was to be the Albert Hotel on the sea front at Weston-super-Mare. A weekend in October was booked there a year later. The cost was 45 shillings a day, with a reduction for children sharing their parents' room. The aim was to share a brief holiday together before winter set in and to enjoy a varied programme of music and games, discussion and family prayers, with an invited speaker to "help us to understand more of God's will in our lives." The fifteen who went were a disappointingly small number as the cryptic reference in the PCC notes suggests: "Council has no reason to regret having encouraged the first parish house party" but welcomes ideas from the "pioneer participants."

The idea lay dormant until 1978 when a long weekend from Friday evening to Sunday afternoon was booked in February of that year at Brunel Manor near Torquay. It was a home Isambard Brunel designed for himself, but never lived in as he died before it was completed. Now it was a Christian holiday centre, set in beautiful Devon countryside. Michael Blunsum, one of St Mary's home grown priests, had just been appointed director of the centre. Whatever the reason, whether it was the warm welcome he and his wife Joan gave to the St Mary's party or the lovely setting, the weekend was a great success and became an annual event.

Other events also helped break down barriers. Summer Day, with its emphasis on sports, replaced the annual Garden Party, and moved to the spreading cedar trees of Stoke Lodge. It was always intended to be a day of fun and fellowship and to be entirely non profit making, but as the stalls and sideshows increased in number there was often a healthy surplus, which over the years bought a variety of things from hymn books to crockery. Further unabashed fun, if competitively fought, was the game of rounders that followed a Parish picnic in the grounds of Blaise Castle every July. In December 1969 coffee was served for the first time after the Family Service and quickly became a popular feature of the morning services, while the Social Committee became active during this period in dreaming up colourful evenings with a Scottish, Elizabethan or Italian flavour that replaced the rather formal annual Wine and Cheese Party. When the first of these events described as an evening 'Country Style' was announced in January 1971 it was suggested that "ladies need not wear high heeled shoes and gentlemen need not wear suits."

While the 'Church Family' grew closer, the nuclear family came under increasing pressure. Family breakdown, separation and divorce became of increasing pastoral concern. It did not just happen in other parishes, it was happening in Stoke Bishop and in St Mary's itself. Within four months of his arrival Roy Henderson was being petitioned by those who were separated or divorced asking "if the Church would be willing to help." The result was an exploratory meeting in the Church Rooms to see what could be done. There is no record of the outcome but the ongoing concern is reflected in the number of sermons that were reprinted in the magazine on the subject of marriage. On one occasion a divorcee wrote a moving account of her own marriage breakup. "Often counselling will be successful," she wrote, "but isn't it silly how we can confide in a perfect stranger some of our closest secrets and yet we have not been able to share them with our life-long partner."

Eventually St Mary's, through the PCC, had to face up to how it was going to respond to the issue of divorce and remarriage in church. In 1988, a request for two Christians, one of whom was divorced, to be married in church brought the matter to a head. After much prayerful discussion the PCC, mindful of balancing compassion for the couple with a commitment to lifelong marriage, upheld an earlier decision not to remarry a divorced person, but to offer an authorised service of 'Prayer and Dedication after Civil Marriage'.

Curates Come and Go

During his ministry Roy Henderson had responsibility for no fewer than eight stipendary curates. They came in all shapes and sizes, some married, some single, some yet to be ordained on arrival. All lived in 7 Little Stoke Road. All brought a richness and variety to the parish, and under Roy Henderson's mindful tutelage all developed in clerical maturity. Nicholas Monk, who had caretakered the interregnum, left to become vicar of All Saints, Swindon in 1969. He was succeeded by Barry Morrison, a young man from Scotland, who to the delight of the vicar had won a rugby blue playing for Cambridge against Oxford in 1965. He continued to play and once preached from the pulpit sporting a black eye. The church had the joy of seeing him ordained, first as deacon then as priest in Bristol Cathedral. He left for St Margaret's, Edgware in 1972.

Next came the Kews, Richard and Rosemary and family. He was curate at St Paul's, Finchley and had never been further than thirty miles from Tring where he was born. That was now to change. On leaving St Mary's in 1976, the Kews crossed the pond where Richard took a post as Associate Rector of the Episcopalian church in Hamilton and Wenham in Massachusetts. His successor was Andrew Daunton-Fear who had been ordained in 1968 in St Paul's Cathedral in Melbourne, Australia, where his father was Archdeacon. During his time at St Mary's he was instrumental in establishing a ministry of healing. He left in 1979 to become rector of the country parish of Thrapston, near Peterborough. William Challis was single when he arrived from St Mary's, Islington, but was married not long after he left St Mary's, Stoke Bishop, in 1981 to take up a teaching post in a new theological college in Burundi in central Africa.

Two family curates were next, Philip Dixon, 1982, and Alex Welby, 1984. Philip had come from St Stephen's, Soundwell, bringing with him a love of music which brushed off on St Mary's. He moved on to become team vicar of St Barnabas, Adeyfield, Hemel Hempstead. Alex Welby joined St Mary's immediately after his ordination. In marked contrast he became vicar of St Stephen's, West Bowling, Bradford, a parish with a strong Asian population.

Roy Henderson's last curate was Stewart Jones, a Scot with a talent for mimicry. He was still to be ordained when he settled in the parish in 1988 with wife, Sue, and daughter, Naomi. Sue was severely disabled with multiple sclerosis and Stewart's ministry was overshadowed by the agony of watching his wife get progressively worse. The church shared in the family's ordeal and embraced them during the last agonising weeks of Sue's life. She died in August 1990. Throughout, Stewart's faith overcame the anger he sometimes felt and the church rejoiced when he remarried and was appointed vicar of St Luke's, Brislington in 1992, the parish which had given St Mary's two of its vicars, Sydney Worters and Norman Hulbert.

Young People

The curate ran Contact. This seemed to be the rule of thumb and the fortunes of the St Mary's youth group seemed variously to reflect the enthusiasms of the current curate. The group was established early in Roy Henderson's ministry. From the outset it was designed with a strong spiritual input as distinct from being simply a youth club. Stoke Bishop already had a thriving youth club at the time. In February 1968 forty young people between 14 and 21 crowded into a cellar of one of their parents' houses in Downleaze for a successful launch. The group met fortnightly on Sunday evenings for "coffee and chat, singing, a short talk from a speaker followed by a discussion." Social and sporting activities took place outside the Sunday meeting.

By 1973 the group was meeting three nights a week and was tackling "pressing social and spiritual issues", such as the Irish problem and drug taking. There were trips abroad and St Mary's regularly fielded a team in the Bishop's Cup, a night-time outward bound event that seemed invariably to take place in pitch black and heavy mud.

As with any youth group there were the occasional problems. Numbers fell off and the group had to be revitalised. Early in 1975 it was closed down altogether as a result of damage caused by rowdy and drunken behaviour and re-launched later in the year. In 1984 the group was flourishing with forty members.

It is interesting to note that the original group included twenty-one year olds. During this period there were several attempts to target the 18-30 age group. This proved elusive as the numbers tended to be small and transitory, being either students at the halls of residence or those returning to their parents' home during the holidays. Young people who could afford to live in the parish were few in number. Andrew Daunton-Fear launched the first 18-30 meeting in February 1977 with a 'pancake party'.

The younger age groups were a different matter. Children filled the Church Rooms on a Sunday to an extent that serious accommodation problems were being reported. Families in Stoke Bishop were often three or four children large and when a creche too was provided every available space was now filled with children ranging from 0 to 14. The old Sunday School image gradually gave way to a friendlier face. On 8 September 1968 Sunday School was renamed 'The Mariners'. The sexes were no longer segregated and classes became smaller. Two years later Roy Henderson launched and ran 'Adventurers', a holiday club at Easter. Its success made it a regular event. In 1972, through the initiative of Richard Kew, St Mary's joined Pathfinders, a loosely based federation of bible classes for children starting out in secondary school.

In 1973 a suggestion from Anni Davey and a group of mothers from Trinity Theological College led the PCC to discuss setting up a Play Group for 3-5 year olds. It started the next year for three mornings a week. Ten years on it was running daily, and while it was open to all children, its teachers could write, "We aim to carry through to our children and their mothers the life and work of the Church in Stoke Bishop." In October 1976 a mums and toddlers group was started. St Mary's could now offer a Christian education for every age group.

Bells, Organ and Amplification

If you bought a house near a church you had to put up with its bells. While the occasional complaint was voiced, it was clear that on the whole the parish loved its bells. This was clearly demonstrated in

October 1977 when the vicar launched a fund raising appeal to raise £8500 to re-cast the bells "in a lighter peal which will be more suitable for the built up area we have become." The next month he could write with gratitude that over £5000 had been given or covenanted in sixteen days! The whole sum had been given by the end of the year. Yet the parish must have gasped when a mere two months later he announced that the organ must be rebuilt and that it would cost £18000. Rescue came in the form of the trustees of the Dame Violet Wills Will Trust who agreed to pay for the work in its entirety.

The bells were recast at the Whitechapel Foundry in London and rung in their new form at Harvest Festival on Sunday 1 October. They retained the Latin verses from the 150th Psalm of the original bells and in addition were inscribed as follows:

Treble In thankfulness for all ringers of this church
Two In thankfulness for all vergers of this church
Three In joyful memory of James Benet Bennett 1977
Four In joyful memory Winifred Mary Codrington 1977
Five In joyful memory Henry Louis Bothamley 1976
Tenor In joyful memory William Edwards George 1921

The last named donated the first tenor in 1874.

As the bells rang out the organ was dismantled. After 70 years it had worn out. The process of deterioration ironically was accelerated by the much welcomed installation of central heating in 1969. The natural materials were susceptible to over-drying, cracking and splitting. In the restoration, the old mechanical action was replaced by an electrical one. The new organ was played at Choral Evensong on Ash Wednesday and, at a service of dedication on Sunday 4 March 1979, a plaque in honour of Dame Violet Wills was unveiled. Roy Massey, the organist of Hereford Cathedral, gave an opening recital the following month.

The other great aural change during this period was the introduction of microphones into the church during services. Commonplace as amplification is today, in 1972, when it was first introduced, it was done tentatively on a trial period only. "It should," the PCC noted, "aid preachers, readers and speakers although it is certainly not necessary for the vicar and Mr Kew who can be heard throughout the church by all normal ears." At the same time a tape-recorder was purchased to record the sermons. A questionnaire returned a positive verdict and amplification was installed permanently using the bequest of Richard Hope-Miles. A loop for the hard of hearing was integrated with the system in 1989. The system itself enjoyed numerous modifications and improvements until the wardens' pew began to resemble a soundmixer's desk in a recording studio. In 1974 amplification was extended to the church rooms.

The expanding sound technology was to a large extent driven by the needs of the new music worship groups which made their appearance during this period. Christian music began to reflect the rhythms and electronic sounds of popular music. Guitars, acoustic to begin with, and later electric, were introduced. Across the wider church tensions arose between the new music and the traditional hymn based choral tradition. St Mary's was not free of these tensions. Some welcomed the new music, others abhorred it. But it was here to stay, and naturally it had a greater appeal to the young and was to play a strong role in making the evening services attractive to them.

Philip Dixon, once himself an organist and choir master, had a great love of the new songs and brought with him an enthusiasm for introducing them. He also had a passion for the music of Taize. On Sunday 3 October 1982 at 7.45 p.m. he launched 'Festival Night', which marked the first serious appearance of the new music. It was described as "music with the curate and Contact." Sixty people attended. It quickly became a popular monthly event. Around the same time Pauline Quintanilla formed the 'St Mary's Music Makers' a singing group which specialised in the new songs. Initially brought together to sing at 'Festival Night', it eventually became part of the Family Service.

In the same year, the choir, which hitherto had only sung at the 11.15 service now transferred to the earlier service. It had become increasingly difficult to recruit young choristers as children preferred to come with their parents to the 'Family Service.' So the two traditions were now to co-exist within the same service. Familiarity with the new songs was helped by the introduction of a new hymn book which printed the most popular ones at the back. The music group itself grew in technological sophistication, plugging itself into the sound system, adding more microphones and finally introducing a keyboard synthesiser.

Finances

The period was characterised by the twin economic evils of inflation and unemployment. These were to have an ongoing and adverse effect on the church's finances. Treasurers have never had it easy but trying to balance books during soaring inflation proved a particularly arduous task.

A simple indicator was the price of the magazine. In January 1971, a year after decimalisation, the price rose from 2.5p to 4p, the first increase since 1957. In 1992 the price was 40p, a staggering nine hundred percent increase. As costs soared the over-riding concern of the PCC was to maintain the level of support to the charities and missionary societies it helped. This was made difficult by the increased sum St Mary's paid each year to the diocese which went towards paying clergy a basic minimum wage. This equality in salaries was designed to reduce the gap between richly and poorly endowed parishes. The effect was to increase the financial burden placed on perceived wealthy parishes like Stoke Bishop.

In 1973 the Easter Offering which had always been the personal gift to the vicar was now deducted from his annual stipend, thus reducing the amount the diocese had to pay him. "This means," he said, "that if you are not so generous in future, I personally may not suffer, but the church in this diocese certainly will." In 1976 the diocesan quota rose by £1500 on the previous year. In January 1979 an increase of 24% was announced.

In April 1978 Roy Henderson wrote on the scourge of unemployment. With an election imminent he argued that "we should not accept the concept that unemployment is necessary if our economy is to avoid inflation ..... The Bible makes it plain that work was part of God's gracious will for our good and blessing *(Genesis 2.15).* To be denied the chance to work is to be made less than the human beings God intended us to be." Recession followed inflation. Stoke Bishop did not escape the ravages of unemployment. The professional classes - lawyers, accountants, bank managers - were not immune. A major part of the clergy's ministry was now to those for whom unemployment had once seemed an impossibility. It was another blow to the church's beleagured finances.

Treasurers sought ways to persuade people to maximise their giving and to break the long held tradition of placing the coin in the collecting bag. Covenants, planned giving through envelopes, bankers orders were introduced with regular talks on tax benefits available to the church. But whatever they called it - 'deficit budget', 'budget of opportunity' - treasurers could not escape the forces outside their control. Occasionally the books were balanced but more often a gift day was held towards the end of the year to encourage people to make up the deficit. Thankfully, God provided.

If the money hadn't come in, it would have been the missionaries in the field who would have suffered. St Mary's continued to support a large number of men and women at home and abroad. There was Pat Bennett, a nurse in Bollophpur Hospital in East Pakistan. The hospital got caught up in the civil war that brought about the creation of the new state of Bangladesh in 1971. The magazine carried Pat Bennett's dramatic accounts of the horror of civil conflict. She, like Sue Woodcock in Bolivia, was a mission partner attached to St Mary's. Others came from the congregation. John and Philippa Prosser went to Paraguay, Kevin and Penny Lawes to Dabou on the Ivory Coast, Margaret Burkett and Diana Austin to the Cameroons, Gillian Minogue to Hong Kong, Judith Wotton and Jamie Forbes to Pakistan.

A man who straddled home and abroad was Korky Davey, a dynamic and charismatic figure whose work captured the imagination of the church. After studying at Trinity Theological College, Korky and his wife Anni settled in the parish and the PCC adopted them when they opened a regional branch of Open Air Campigners in the Bristol area in 1977. The latter was an evangelical Christian organisation that started in Australia. Its founder, E.P. Field, developed new methods of preaching in the open air, using visual aids and in particular a large sketch board on which the Gospel appeared with deft strokes of the paint brush. The movement reached England in 1965, its representative preaching to the crowds on Brighton sea front. St Mary's gave Korky's work its blessing. The congregation listened entranced to his regular appearances in the pulpit as his bearded animated figure got into its stride describing O.A.C.'s work in Bristol, across the south west and further afield in Greece, Spain and Albania. Soon the organisation was receiving the largest contribution from the church's annual giving.

Church Fabric - Changes and Effect

Welcome though the installation in 1969 of the new central heating system was, it had, as we have seen, deleterious effects on the organ. It was also oil fired and when the world was hit by a series of oil crises in the seventies, creating serious shortages, what was once the cheapest form of fuel now became expensive and scarce. Before it was converted to gas in 1980, economies had to be made. In 1975 evening services were moved to the church rooms from January to Easter to save fuel. "While we shall miss our church building for worship, we may find there are other compensations." This was to prove so. Many found there a more welcoming atmosphere and ideal for the informal services that were introduced later.

Another experiment in worship happened, too, because the church was out of action. In September 1989 the interior of the buiding was completely redecorated in three weeks. For two Sundays a combined morning service was held on the Downs. On the first it rained, although 170 people enjoyed the novelty. "Scovell Whitmore read the lesson carrying his Bible in a plastic bag. James Rex held a large umbrella over the vicar. David Gillett preached: 'Jesus where'er thy people meet - every place is hallowed ground'." After a misty start the second Sunday shone bright and clear. A precedent had been set.

The major change that took place inside the church was the building of a platform in front of the chancel steps. The numbers going forward at the Family Service Communion, including children to be blessed, necessitated two and sometimes three points at which people received the elements. In 1991 the PCC went ahead with its plans to extend an area on a level with the choir stalls by building a platform out into the nave. Two rows of front pews were removed and the whole area from high altar to platform covered in a new blue carpet. During communion a table was placed on the platform enabling the whole church to get a view of the celebrant. At other times the platform acted as a stage.

Church Rooms Extension

When a church complained of lack of space it was often a sign of healthy growth. This was true of St Mary's in the seventies. The increase in the numbers attending Sunday school during the morning service strained the capacity of the Church Rooms. The PCC felt it wrong that some children should be taught in what amounted to 'cupboards'. In 1969 a committee was set up to investigate 'in depth' and see whether an extension was necessary. Whatever their conclusion nothing seems to have been done.

Matters were made worse when the choir moved from the 11.15 service to the Family Service. There was no room for them to robe. As a result they had to squeeze into the churchwardens' vestry in the church causing chaos at the start and end of services. In the Church Rooms the main entrance was being used as a creche causing congestion when the congregation came down for coffee, to say nothing of the danger of small children being trampled on. Roy Henderson warned that numbers might have to be limited.

In 1984 the church architect was asked to draw up plans. He came up with three - one was to extend the church vestries, the other two involved building additional space beside the Hulbert Room at the end of the main church hall. The favoured plan was to extend the Church Rooms by enlarging the Hulbert Room, which could be divided into smaller rooms by a partition, and building an adjacent smaller room at the end of the hall.

At their December meeting the PCC decided to put the proposals, estimated at £70000, to the congregation. A period of consultation took place. There were strongly held views that such a sum should not be spent on 'ourselves'. But when a vote was taken

75% of the congregation was in favour. On 8 March 1985 a half night of prayer was held and on the following Saturday morning the PCC met to make a decision. They "decided by a substantial majority to ask the architect to seek planning permission and obtain competitive tenders for the proposed extension."

An Appeal Committee was set up and under the leadership of its imaginative chairman, James Rex, began the long haul to raise the money. It was launched on Sunday 15 September, preceeded by another half night of prayer. The sum to be raised was now announced as £75000. Harvest Sunday was earmarked as a Day of Dedication for covenants, pledges and gifts of money. While it was acknowleged that this would be the principal source of revenue, it was hoped that a lot of fun and fellowship would be had along the way, with the first event announced being an auction complete with professional auctioneer.

Sixty six thousand pounds was raised in two and a half months. But shoals were ahead. When he announced the proposals Roy Henderson had said: "They terrify me .... We have a God who never allows us to settle back into an easy and comfortable security." How true his words were. One month after building work began in April 1986, he had to announce a substantial increase on the original estimates. This was brought about by additional planning and safety requirements and amendments to the original plan which now included a servery and toilet facilities and a ramp to provide disabled access.

Although further consultation was held, the vicar felt they were building for the future. "I hope we shall not fail in our courage and vision, even if it is going to mean additional sacrifice and hard work to achieve the objective to which we believe God has been calling us." The figure one year after the Appeal was launched stood at £92000 (it was to finish at £94500), but the parish carried on in faith. Under 'Jim' Rex's benign cajoling the money raising events went on unabated. There were talent auctions, car washing sessions, concerts, jazz and Victorian evenings, a 'buy a brick' scheme and most effective of all a walking festival, which raised £3000 in sponsorship. There were walks of varying lengths but the most ambitious was a marathon completed by a few hardy persons including the vicar.

On Sunday 16 November 1986 the new extension was formally opened by Roy Henderson's predecessor, Leslie Williams. In his Christmas letter the vicar wrote joyfully of a "great occasion." There was a united service at which Leslie Williams preached. "During the service we could see and hear the rain beating down on the windows, but by the time we came to the final hymn it had ceased and the procession down Mariners Drive to the Extension took place in the dry." There was fruit punch and a large cake cut by the wife of another previous vicar Canon Mike Hulbert. In the afternoon the bell ringers completed a successful peal. The newly enlarged Hulbert Room (after Canon Hulbert) retained its name and the smaller room commemorated Frank and Joan Evans who had been churchwarden and lay reader respectively. Joan had only recently died of cancer.

Teaching, Outreach and Ecumenism

The results of mission are often difficult to quantify. Any lasting effects may only be known years after the event. During Roy Henderson's ministry a number of initiatives were undertaken to reach the wider community both inside and outside the church. Early on in his ministry in October 1968 he established Thursday as a regular evening in the week for the parish to meet "for fellowship, for discussing the implications of some of the big issues before the churches today and for a deepening of our understanding of the faith in order that we may be able to present it more effectively to those with whom we come into contact." The first meeting was Harvest Supper.

The second was held in Westbury Baptist Church and was part of a series on other Christian Churches. It was a fitting venue as the month before saw the opening of the new Baptist Church in Reedly Road, the first new church to be built close to St Mary's (although just outside the parish) since the demolition of the Congregational Church in Sneyd Park in 1962. It had also hosted the first united service of the Westbury Council of Churches. St Mary's supported the venture but

Four years after the opening of the Church Rooms Extension in Jauary 1990, a large beech tree crashed onto the roof during the Thursday Lunch. No one was hurt but the roof was badly damaged

Roy Henderson in the vestry officiating at the signing of the marriage register. The couple are Philip and Katherine (nee Burkett) Thomas

still held Evensong at the same time. Although it was felt ecumenism was to be encouraged it reflected its less than enthusiastic support for the fledgling Westbury Council. Part of the reason was St Mary's geographic isolation at the edge of the Council's area, which made it difficult to share fellowship. Roy Henderson himself was a champion of unity and in 1972 when the proposed Anglican - Methodist union failed in General Synod he was greatly saddened and urged a "greater commitment to and support for the Westbury Council of Churches." It happened but only in fits and starts.

Within church new ventures started. In April 1970 through a combined initiative of Mothers' Union and Wives' Fellowship monthly teas for the elderly were arranged. Volunteer car drivers were organised and eight people came to the first meeting. In this small way the 'Wednesday Circle' was born. Two years on eighty people were attending. As well as tea there were speakers to entertain and outings in summer. In 1981 the net was spread more widely with the launch of the weekly Parish Lunch. Thursday became a regular date when for a modest sum "mums and dads, grandparents, brothers and sisters" could enjoy a simple meal "joining together as the whole family of the church."

In 1987 two members of the congregation, Chris Rouse and Mary Henwood, came back from Taize inspired by what they had experienced there. They held two supper parties at which they introduced the ideas of silence and meditative singing. The curate, Alex Welby, was a guest at one and suggested they form a regular group. Thus the 'Bible Meditation and Prayer Fellowship' came into being which provided an opportunity to explore the fruits of silence and meditative prayer. In 1989 the group held the first of what was to become an annual occasion - a Quiet Day. It chose a title that summed up its essence - 'Be still and know that I am God'.

There were a number of missions in the parish during the period. For ten weeks during the autumn of 1975 St Mary's proclaimed 'New Life in '75'. Highlight was the evening service of 9 November when Cliff Richard, international rock star and committed Christian, filled the church to bursting as he led the congregation in a celebration of Christian music. Four years later a joint venture by all the churches in the Stoke Bishop, Westbury and Henleaze areas, known as Contact '79, was planned for the autumn. It ended with a rousing service at the Colston Hall attended by a thousand people, with the Reverend Dr Donald English giving the final address.

But by far the biggest, and probably the most influential, event was 'Mission England' in May 1984. American evangagelist, Billy Graham toured Great Britain and a number of gruelling 8 day missions were held in football stadiums up and down the country. Ashton Gate in Bristol was chosen as the venue for the south west and St Mary's was one of a number of local churches recruited to provide the support. Preparations began eighteen months earlier, through house churches, services and special courses. Members of St Mary's were trained to be counsellors and stewards and were commissioned to visit people in the parish and invite them to come on the special St Mary's bus to Ashton Gate.

This was high profile Christianity. On the final night 38000 filled the stadium. On one occasion, in response to Billy Graham's invitation to commit their lives to Christ, 4000 went forward. It left indelible impressions on those involved. "The clapping hit us like a tidal wave as we sat down, relieved and pleased. We really did feel we were singing for the Lord as the songs went up into the skies" *(Anne Davey, choir, aged 14).* "Another concern was would I be required? Were people going to come forward in hundreds as expected? ..... they indeed came forward, not in hundreds, but thousands, and I was needed"*(Roger Harvey, counsellor).* According to parishioner Bill Burkett, who was on the local co-ordinating committee, there were 120 people referred to St Mary's for follow up. In his letter to thank those who helped, Bill noted also that St Mary's "had been selected to act as hosts and providers of refreshments before the meetings to the 'nobs and notables'". Two results of the mission were the creating of a network of prayer triplets and the establishment of a regular Christian Basics Course to nurture new Christians.

New Curates

When in February 1982 Roy Henderson announced that Stewart Jones was leaving to be vicar of St Luke's, Brislington, he also explained that he would not be replaced. With a shortage of curates available, the Bishop had to re-assess his priorities. In the current situation he felt that St Mary's could fend for itself. It had many gifted lay people, it had staff from nearby Trinity Theological College worshipping there and over the years it had grown a number of its own curates. Roy Henderson had a gift for training, and, while he was responsible for the progress of the young curates assigned to him, he was also very supportive of those in the congregation who felt a calling to the ministry later in their lives. Either in retirement or while still at work it was hoped these non-stipendary ministers would provide much needed assistance to the full-time ministry. On 30 June 1974 Reg Bell, who had retired from his engineering business, was ordained deacon at Bristol Cathedral and ordained priest the following year. In his footsteps came Michael Blunsum, a bank manager (1975), Ben Pullen, who worked for Bristol Council (1977), and James Rex, a retired civil engineer (1989).

Unfortunately for St Mary's this process never proved to be the godsend it promised as invariably, for one reason or another, the new clergy moved on soon after they had been ordained. The Bishop was not in favour of the new ordinands staying in the church they had worshipped in and he sent Reg Bell to Horfield Parish Church and Ben Pullen to St Alban's, Westbury Park, although Reg Bell came back in 1978 when he retired as a NSM. Michael Blunsum, as we have seen, took over the running of Brunel Manor, near Torquay. James Rex stayed long enough to get accustomed to the idea of the clerical collar. When he asked his colleague, Stewart Jones, how he should view his job, quick as a flash Jones replied: "Through your glasses." Crossing the line from congregation to clergy was a trip into the unknown that had its rewards and its frustrations. In 1991 James Rex secured a job in the diocese of Chichester when he and his wife moved to Sussex to be closer to their family. The next year Stewart Jones left, leaving the parish without a curate. Another member of the congregation was starting out on her training as a NSM, but she had three years to go.

Women

When Christine Froude responded to the call to embrace the ministry she did not know whether she would ever be able to become a full priest. In 1992 when she was selected for training the Church of England still only recognised women as deacons. If full priesthood became a reality Christine was conscious that she would be a guinea pig in the movement for women's ordination. For St Mary's too the issue was no academic one. But, through careful nurturing from their vicar, the congregation was prepared.

Acceptance of women in positions of authority in St Mary's was slow and sometimes reluctant through this period. In April 1972 at the Annual Meeting six 'sideswomen' were elected for the first time. A report in the magazine was less than enthusiastic. "And, believe it or not, 'Women's Lib.' insisted on by ladies at the meeting, with somewhat lukewarm male backing, despite a female opposition voice or two in favour of leaving collections at St Mary's to the splendid corps of male sidesmen, provided a lively finale." Although women had been elected to the PCC for a number of years, it was not until 1986 that St Mary's had its first woman churchwarden. In that year Margaret Sellin was unanimously elected. She proved a popular choice and quickly showed she was eminently qualified for the job. It was in the family, as both her parents had been wardens, her father, Arthur Carter, serving under Leslie Williams. Her success established the precedent whereby St Mary's alternated its wardens by gender.

But a woman priest was a greater challenge. In 1977 Roy Henderson wrote that the Church of England was not yet ready for the ordination of women but by 1981 it had stated that it saw no theological objection to women being ordained. As the years went by, without being overtly didactic, he continued to prepare the way for acceptance. "Or does the solution (to a shortage of clergy) lie in the ordination of women to the priesthood? Is that what God is calling us to do by allowing the numbers of men called to diminish?" "Paul wrote to the Galatians: 'There is neither male nor female, for you are all one in Christ Jesus." In October 1990 as the General Synod prepared to vote on the issue the following February he held a special

Saturday morning meeting in the Church Rooms. He made it clear how important the opinion of the ordinary churchgoer was. It would first be discussed in the Deanery Synods, before being voted on in the Diocesan Synods. A majority of the 43 dioceses had to be in favour before it could even go forward to the General Synod. He lucidly put the case for and against ordination allowing everyone present to make up their own mind. When Christine Froude told him she was considering ordination he expressed surprise, having no idea that she was considering such a step, but he was overjoyed that she wanted to serve God in this way.

From Trinity to Canterbury

Few parishes can count themselves as lucky as St Mary's was in 1972 when Trinity Theological College was established within its parish boundaries. At the time there were three Anglican colleges in Bristol - Clifton, Tyndale Hall and Dalton House with St Michael's. Clifton was already established in Stoke House off Stoke Hill and the previous year Roy Henderson had been appointed Director of Pastoral Studies, where he lectured once a week. It was proposed to create a united college on the Stoke Bishop site and the new Trinity Theological College came into being under the principalship of the Reverend Alec Motyer, vicar of St Luke's, West Hamstead, in London.

St Mary's benefited from this institution in a number of ways. The congregation enjoyed regular sermons from Trinity's lecturers, a number of whom worshiped with their families and were able to make a valuable contribution to parish life. Students also adopted St Mary's as their parish church. Many came from abroad and the church got used to seeing faces of different colours in its midst. Finally Roy Henderson always had the comfort of knowing he could call on his colleagues at Trinity to preach or lead a service when needed. As Trinity grew and developed it bought a number of houses in the area and Trinity families found themselves part of the Stoke Bishop community, while its buildings and landscaped grounds provided a perfect location for quiet days and summer fetes.

The College's second principal was the vicar of St Nicholas, Durham. His name was George Carey. He took up his appointment in 1981 and he was to have a symbiotic relationship with St Mary's and its vicar. He preached regularly from the pulpit and led the Parish Weekend at Brunel Manor in 1984. His wife, Eileen, sat on the PCC and his children were involved in the leadership of Contact. At the same time Roy Henderson's links with Trinity were made firmer when he was appointed Chairman of Trinity College Council, the College's governing body, in May 1983.

In 1985 Roy Henderson made a portentous decision. Five years earlier he had been elected to the General Synod. Although he recognised the importance of the role, his heart was not really in it. In a report on his first session he wrote: "It is good to be back pastoring and teaching again in the parish." Thus when he decided not to seek re-election in 1985, he nominated George Carey in his place. Two years later the latter was appointed Bishop of Bath and Wells and Roy Henderson had the honour of preaching at his enthronement in Southwark Cathedral. When the news came through in August 1990 that he was to be the next Archbishop of Canterbury, St Mary's felt justly proud that in some small way it had contributed to the making of a primate.

Sabbatical and Pastoral Leadership Team

One of the last services George Carey rendered to St Mary's before departing to the moated palace at Wells was to give advice and counsel to clergy and wardens during the Vicar's sabbatical. In May 1987 Roy Henderson announced that he would be taking study leave for three months between September and December. He had been in the parish for nearly twenty years and the Bishop thought a sabbatical rest was long overdue. During those twenty years he had not only pastored his flock zealously but had taken on many pastoral duties outside the parish.

We have touched on his work for Trinity and his election to the General Synod. But for six years from 1973 he was Rural Dean for Westbury and Severnside, which involved responsibility for the pastoral care of the clergy in the deanery. In the wider field he was chairman of all the Church Pastoral Aid Society's Patronage Trusts. These were responsible for appointing clergy to over 500 livings in the Church of England. It was an important post and involved a monthly meeting in London on a Thursday. This meant leaving home before breakfast and rushing back to be in time for the start of St Mary's Night. In 1980 he was elected Honorary Canon at Bristol Cathedral and in 1985 appointed Chairman of the House of Clergy until his retirement. Also in 1985 he served on the Crown Appointments Commission, which included the Archbishops of Canterbury and York, the body involved in recommending the next Bishop of Bristol.

So it was with some relief that he set off in September on his study leave. He had set himself the task of looking at how other churches with memberships of over 500 "pastor their people." He knew that St Mary's would soon be losing its full time curate, nor would it have a verger after the current verger, Peter Bilby, retired. He needed to have in place a structure that provided for a greater lay involvement in the running of the church. At their Away Day held before he left the PCC explored the most effective pattern of ministry for the future. It concluded that the New Testament pattern of leadership was "a group or team of people working together rather than a single leader."

During his three months away he visited 15 churches from Lancaster in the north to Maidstone in the east. He came back with a frank and challenging report. "The biggest problem (in a large church)," he wrote, "often lay with the vicar. He had probably come from a much smaller congregation where he had been able to cope with most of the pastoral work himself, but there is no way he can do it in a large congregation, and if he tries he is probably heading for a breakdown." The solution was often some form of collective leadership involving clergy and lay people. Another problem was overcoming the perception that "if the clergy have not done it, the church has not done it."

Through 1988 he prepared the congregation for the introduction of a Pastoral Leadership Team. The aim was to give "me more eyes, more ears, more hours and more gifts than I can have on my own." It would "exercise general oversight and pastoral care for the work of St Mary's, bring ideas to the PCC and implement the policy decisions of the Council." There were to be six members responsible for Worship and Prayer, Pastoral Care, Mission, Teaching and Fellowship, Youth, and Administration and Literature." The team, to serve for a limited period of three years, was to enable work to be carried out, but not to do it all themselves. The congregation was invited to suggest suitable names. The first six, chosen by the vicar, were approved by the PCC in June and commissioned with prayer at the Family Communion Service on 10 July.

For a vicar coming up to retirement at the end of twenty four years in the same parish the support and encouragement of the PLT was of great comfort. It met weekly for prayers followed by a pastoral breakfast and monthly in the evenings for a longer business meeting. Although it lost two members quite soon after its establishment it soon settled into an efficient working routine and was well established when Roy Henderson announced that Stewart Jones would not be replaced when he left. At the same time he set up training for a further layer of lay involvement. With the help of David Gillett, the new principal of Trinity, he prepared a number of the congregation to lead services and intercessions. He also trained couples to take over part of the marriage preparation and baptismal welcoming. A third group was trained to take Holy Communion to the residents of an ever growing number of nursing and residential homes in the parish.

Retirement

At the Annual Parochial Church Meeting on 12 April 1992, Roy Henderson announced his retirement. His last service would be Sunday 18 October, the day before his 65th birthday. He and his wife planned to settle on the South Devon coast and he hoped to continue his ministry in the diocese of Exeter where he had been first ordained, in between a regular round of golf. The parish prepared a great send off and held a party on the Friday before his departure, fittingly, at Trinity College, in the newly built conference room. Most touching was the assembled cast of curates who had passed through Roy Henderson's hands during his twenty four years. Bill Burkett, who had known him for the whole of his ministry, paid tribute to his years in Stoke Bishop. "The outstanding feature of Roy's ministry," he said, "in a time of uncertainty and hesitation, and in some cases loss of nerve in the church generally, has been his outstanding biblical teaching." He went on with tongue in cheek, "Some people have said that the greatest cross a vicar has to bear is his PCC. I can vouch for the fact that he has very gently and diplomatically allowed the PCC to do exactly what he wanted." But the tribute that particularly affected him was one contained in a letter he received from Lambeth Palace acknowledging "his rich and fruitful ministry at St Mary's (and his) splendid and deep teaching which has been an inspiration and joy to so many" and going on to say, "perhaps I need to remind you that it may well be the case that I have you to thank for my becoming Archbishop of Canterbury!"

CHAPTER SIX

(by Keith Sheather)

1992 - 2000

As he gets closer to the present, the historian finds it is increasingly difficult to tease out the themes and meanings in events. The remainder of this history must inevitably be subjective and the author leaves it to future historians to identify and interpret the moments of significance in the concluding years of this current history.

Interregnum

There was no one waiting in the wings to be offered the living at Stoke Bishop when Roy Henderson retired. Barry Rogerson, the Bishop of Bristol, within whose patronage the church fell, suggested that the vacancy be advertised nationally. The PCC prepared its statement as to the nature of the vacancy and the particular qualities they were looking for in the person who was to fill it. At the same time they appointed two of its members who would be responsible, together with the bishop, for selecting the new incumbent. As was customary this duty fell to the churchwardens.

St Mary's was fortunate to have in the posts two people with complementary abilities. Mary Burkett had been a member of the church since arriving in the parish in 1947. There was little she did not know about the workings of St Mary's. Her wise and spiritual counsel and her long memory were great assets. David Speedyman had a mastery of detail and an instinctive grasp of administrative procedures. It was a crucial partnership and brought about a smooth transition to the new incumbency. Of considerable help were the new structures that Roy Henderson had put in place before he left for securing greater lay participation. The Pastoral

Leadership Team covered every area of church life and was responsible for involving large numbers of the congregation in conducting services, leading prayers and drawing up rotas. As Roy Henderson said before he left, "It is no bad thing for you all to discover just how much you can do for yourself." The church did indeed surprise itself.

Spiritually the parish was in good hands. Trinity, in the persons of its principal, Canon David Gillett, and the Reverend Dr Philip Jenson, took the church under its wing and treated the congregation as its surrogate flock. The Reverend Reg Bell was called out of retirement, again, and officiated at weddings and funerals. Invitations went out to a myriad of guest preachers who had a connection with St Mary's and people were entertained to a wide range of sermon styles, including former curate Stewart Jones' inimitable impersonation of Peter Sellars' comic creation, Inspector Clouseau.

The interregnum began with a well attended half night of prayer. That support was of great comfort to the wardens as they embarked on the selection process. The advert drew over 40 enquiries from Britain and overseas. These resulted in 22 firm applications from which the bishop drew up a short list of 5. The chosen applicants, with their families, were invited to Bristol for an interview and a chance to meet members of the PCC and to have a look around the parish. After two days of scrutiny on both sides a unanimous decision was reached. For the second time in its history St Mary's new vicar would come from overseas.

The New Vicar

The Reverend David Ritchie, at the time of his appointment in November 1992, was Anglican chaplain of three English churches in Switzerland: All Saints, Vevey, St Peter's, Chateau D'Oex and the English Church at Villars, where incidentally he had spent three years at an international school as a boy. He and his family lived at Vevey, famed for its association with Charlie Chaplin and the chocolate manufacturer, Nestle. After eight years in Switzerland, and with four young children to educate, David felt, at 44, it was time that he and his wife, Elisabeth, or Lis as she was to be known, moved back to England. So it was "with great joy", he wrote in his first letter to the parish, " that we responded to the bishop's invitation to accept the living of St Mary's..... I was glad to see how near the church is to the vicarage. In my work here in Switzerland our furthest church is 35 miles away - and I have never been very skilful at putting on snow chains in blizzard conditions!"

Quick though the appointment was, the new vicar was not able to move in so quickly. Firstly the vicarage was out of commission until March, while a new heating system was installed and the house decorated. Then David Ritchie himself made a flying visit to explain over a PLT breakfast of coffee and cornflakes that, due to family reasons and Bishop Barry's full diary, he would not be with the parish until July. As one writer in the magazine put it: "We had been conducting our business as though we were athletes in the 100 metres, but (now) we must adopt the more measured pace of the 400 metres." It was a blow but the network of people able to provide help and support was growing all the time and the congregation was increasingly buoyed up by the approaching date of 20 July set for David Ritchie's induction and collation.

New Approaches

In his first article in the magazine David Ritchie thanked everyone for the warm welcome he and his family had received. "I know", he wrote, "that these past nine months have been a time of real growth in the life of St Mary's as individuals have taken on new responsibilities and perhaps been surprised at how well the church has run without a vicar! Indeed one member of St Mary's recently said to me 'what are you going to do?'" It was an encouraging start, but that support had to be ongoing if the new situation - a vicar without a full time curate - was going to be viable in a church the size of St Mary's. David Gillett warned that there was a danger that after the great effort of the interregnum it would be all too easy to breathe a sigh of relief that the vicar was in place and to let him get on with it. That could no longer happen. Fortunately the structure of a team of pastoral leaders gave the vicar considerable help in the early months. But no one fully appreciated the enormity of the task ahead. It was a sea change in people's minds that had to be effected. The fact that the vicar could no longer be everywhere at all times was easier to say than to understand. The first years of David Ritchie's ministry were to see a profound change in the life of St Mary's, worked out in often painful circumstances.

Demise of the PLT

In February 1994, the vicar outlined his concept of a shared leadership. He paid tribute to the support he had received from the PLT while settling in and saw its continued support as an essential part of his ministry. Explaining that there were too many tasks for a vicar to undertake by himself, it was vital they be shared around. "I find it thrilling," he said, "to find the church filled every Sunday - and yet I also find it an awesome responsibility as I realise my accountability before God for the continuing life and witness of St Mary's." Two changes were made in the structure of the group. Responsibility for mission or outreach reverted to the PCC and a Prayer Co-ordinator was brought into the team. But most importantly "the PLT came to the conclusion that I, as vicar, should concentrate on ….teaching and preaching, sacramental and priestly functions, and enabling others to identify their own special call to service." All else would be undertaken by the laity. It was a brave vision.

Yet as time went on relations between the PLT and the PCC became troubled. As had happened in other churches where a similar structure had been set up questions as to the power of the PLT began to be asked. Whereas it was made clear at the beginning that it was not an executive body but one answerable to the PCC and enjoined to carry out its policy decisions, on occasions such niceties became blurred. At the Annual Parochial Church Meeting in 1995 a question was asked as to the "official relationship between the PCC and the PLT." Members of the PLT itself were sometimes confused. To avoid accusations of an inner cabal functioning outside the authority of the PCC, the Pastoral Leadership Team was wound up in June 1995. In its place emerged a Pastoral Support Group. Introducing it David Ritchie made it clear that it had no executive authority, that was the sole prerogative of the churchwardens and the PCC. Its role was to provide "assistance to the vicar in his position within the overall shared ministry of St Mary's." Yet many of the responsibilities of the old PLT were retained - prayer support, helping to seek the spiritual direction of the church, assistance in pastoral care, identifying individuals for particular tasks and undertaking "as directed by the vicar, any tasks which assist him in discharging his responsibilities."

Although executive policy-making was back firmly within the hands of the PCC, a vacuum in the detailed direction of the church's activities was left by the demise of the PLT. A survey revealed that there were over seventy organisations and activities associated with St Mary's, all needing a person or body to look to for advice and guidance. An elaborate committee structure was proposed and adopted by the PCC so that all organisations would come under a committee and so have a direct relationship with the PCC. The committees covered worship, pastoral care, Christian growth, outreach, mission, children and young people, communications, fabric, finance, social and personnel. The chairpeople were not necessarily members of the PCC, but each committee had to have two PCC members sitting on it to ensure its accountability.

Inevitably there were teething problems. Questions of overlap had to be sorted out. Some committees took time to get started. Enthusiasm meant that ideas often outran the people available to carry them out. As they proceeded there was an equal danger that they became mere talking shops. But, unquestionably, they helped the vicar in keeping the parish afloat.

Women's Ordination

During the interregnum women's ordination finally became a reality. David Gillett was in the General Synod when the crucial vote was taken. In the magazine he wrote: "There was much emotion after the debate itself, although the result was, as is customary, received in silence. Many women deacons on the Synod, and others who had been around the building during the day were understandably overcome with joy and relief." One who shared these emotions was undoubtedly Christine Froude. She was coming to the end of her three years training and was eagerly awaiting ordination. As part of her training she had to undergo a three month practical placement. She asked to be assigned to St Mary's, Olveston, near the Severn Bridge. The incumbent was the Reverend Anita Thorne, one of the first women in the Bristol Diocese to be made a priest on 13 March 1994. Christine wanted to learn "first hand the gifts and skills women bring to ministry and how these fit together with being a wife and mother."

To the great joy of many in St Mary's the Reverend Christine Froude was ordained deacon on 2 July 1995 at a service in Bristol Cathedral. Although the bishop could have assigned her to any parish in the diocese, she was allowed to stay at St Mary's to give much needed support to the vicar. A year later she was priested, able to give absolution and administer the holy sacraments. She was in no doubt that, while many in St Mary's accepted her wholeheartedly, she knew that, as she put it, "she was at the cutting edge of people's strongly held views." She was prepared for rejection, but it pained her to have individuals refuse to shake her hand or accept communion from her, although she understood the conviction from which such actions flowed. But as her talent for pastoral care and her spiritual vigour became apparent minds changed.

Staff Changes

For David Ritchie having Christine Froude join the staff of St Mary's was a great relief. An illness the preceding winter, in which he had to withdraw from parish duties for two months, showed again how vulnerable the church was. The PCC knew it could expect no help from the diocese and slowly recognised that if it wanted permanent staff it would have to pay for them. It experimented with a youth leader, but it gradually emerged that the real need was for somebody to undertake the day to day administration of the church and the church rooms.

By his own admission David Ritchie was no administrator. Christine Froude's talents were more urgently needed elsewhere. A single secretary working part time had more work than she could cope with. In line with modern business methods it was time to bring in the consultants. For the Anglican church this meant Administry, an independent C of E based organisation, specialising in helping churches run themselves. The man from Administry was called in and after an intensive study of St Mary's working methods made his recommendations. These in essence boiled down to the need to appoint a church manager. As the vicar wrote: "This is not a luxury - but a necessity. Viewed in secular terms, St Mary's is the equivalent of a middle-sized business where good management is essential." Such a person would release the clergy "to concentrate on those tasks for which they were ordained - namely preaching and teaching, pastoral work and prayer." In the early church this is exactly what happened. Acts 6 vv1-7 records how administrative problems relating to the distribution of money to the poor were stopping the apostles preaching God's word. "They chose Stephen, a man full of faith and the Holy Spirit", and six others, to deal with the matter. An advert duly appeared in the magazine - "25 hours per week including Sundays. Salary in the region of £7500."

The successful applicant was Mike Barwell. He and his wife Patsy had just returned from Hong Kong, where Mike had worked as Senior Administrative Officer to the diocese of Hong Kong. He was a true pioneer having little idea of what the job entailed beyond a determination to make the best use of the church's resources to allow the clergy more time for teaching and pastoral work.

Another important staff change came about when the PCC decided the post of verger was no longer viable. The current verger, Peter Bilby, had been with St Mary's for over twenty years. He was a very present figure around the church and one who had the added burden of looking after his wife who was suffering from multiple sclerosis. It had always been made clear that when Peter Bilby retired it was unlikely that he would be replaced. St Mary's was one of only a handful of parishes in the Bristol Diocese still to have a full-time verger, apart from St Mary Redcliffe with its civic responsibilities. After considerable prayer and two extraordinary meetings, clergy, wardens and PCC, with a heavy heart, decided unanimously to make the post of verger at St Mary's redundant. In order to give Peter Bilby as generous a settlement as possible it was required, for legal reasons, that the redundancy notice be carried out in a matter of days.

On Sunday 26 October 1997, an announcement was made at all services to this effect. The shock waves were tangible. There was deep sadness, often expressed in a way that threatened to divide the church. In a milestone sermon that sought to call upon the healing powers of reconciliation, David Gillett went back to the early church and described the dispute between Paul and Barnabas (Acts 15 vv 36-41) over who was to accompany them on their missionary journeys. So bitter became the disagreement that they parted company, and set out to serve God in their separate ways. Sometimes in a church this becomes necessary, he said. A number of worshippers did indeed leave St Mary's to go to other churches. It was a painful episode and one from which the church only slowly began to recover.

Worship, Welcome and Prayer

While the verger affair cast a long shadow over events it should not obscure the many positive things that were happening in St Mary's during this decade. Welcomers, wearing yellow badges, greeted newcomers in the church rooms and introduced them to other members of the congregation. After the 9.45 morning service, two members of a specially trained team were available in the James Chapel to offer prayers for any one who came to them with a personal need.

In 1994 a new church bible was proposed to replace the New English Bible. Favourite with the PCC was the New International Version (NIV), but the Reverend Dr Philip Jenson of Trinity College argued persuasively for the New Revised Standard Version, which was already in use at Trinity. It was, he said, the most accurate translation yet produced and it used inclusive language where the text allowed. As it had only been published in 1989, it was unfamiliar to most and so a trial period was held in which the NRSV alternated with the NIV. It proved easier to read and was finally adopted as the pew bible. It had the practical advantage that the page layout and numbering were the same for the large lectern bible as for the smaller ones in the pews.

New services were started. A family Crib Service was introduced as part of the Christmas services for 1995. It was a great success and became an annual feature. In 1998 attendance was 231. Less successful was the vicar's attempt to bring in a monthly combined service. Like Roy Henderson before him, he had the vision of the whole church worshipping together. It began in a quiet way. Christine Froude introduced the idea in the magazine. "Worship of this sort is always costly but brings the blessing of God's peace which passes all understanding." A quarterly celebratory service was launched at 10.30 on 7 January 1996 followed by a parish lunch in the church rooms. The following year this became monthly. Sadly it never acquired the popularity he had hoped and the experiment was quietly abandoned after a year.

But this was not true of another experiment started around the same time. On a beautiful September's evening in 1996 a good congregation from St Mary's assembled on the Downs near Ivywell Road for an open air service. Those with long memories had recalled with affection the first time it had happened during the re-decoration of the church in 1989. Praising God in the open air had a relaxed immediacy that caught the imagination. Such was its popularity that it became a regular event in the summer. Although the services were often different in character - Holy Communion, a Pets Service and a Songs of Praise - they were all informal, with live music and people sitting on chairs or rugs. The weather was not always kind but the spirits were always high. One of the services preceded the parish picnic and barbecue, which replaced Summer Day as St Mary's main summer gathering.

Fabric - Adornment

On Sunday 10 October 1993, Roy Henderson was invited back to St Mary's to dedicate the first stained glass window to be incorporated in the church for almost fifty years. It was in memory of John Davies, a church warden, who died suddenly on 13 February 1992, aged 48. The glass was placed in the rose window in the north transept over the door to the church rooms. It was the work of Michael Slaughter of Creative Glass in Bristol. Unlike the Victorian windows, it was abstract in design, but used the traditional colours of ruby and blue that radiated the light. The glass itself was mouthblown creating, in the words of the artist, "a vitality and subtlety of both texture and colour that … no machine has yet been able to emulate." At the same time, also in memory of John Davies, an altar frontal was dedicated for the James Chapel. This was the work of 'Poikilia', a group of embroiderers ('poikilia' is Greek for embroidery) who have served the church over a number of years. As well as altar frontals they have created banners and clerical vestments, including a cope and mitre for George Carey when he became Archbishop of Canterbury.

But perhaps the epic contribution to the fabric has been the provision of 250 kneelers undertaken over two years by Monica Jones. The church needed to replace the crumbling moth eaten kneelers. Monica Jones was not happy with standard kit based designs and set about enthusing people with the idea of making their own. At a Parish Weekend she got everyone to try a stitch to see how easy it was. What she created was a time capsule in tapestry. The hundreds of images that now provide a resting place for prayerful knees reflect the interests, concerns, memories and beliefs of St Mary's in 1994. Inside each kneeler is a written text - a bible verse, a prayer or simply what the weather was like.

Fabric - Renovation

In 1995 pieces of masonry started falling off the church tower. There was no danger of it collapsing, but urgent repair work had to be done. This involved replacing crumbling columns with new stone. At the same time the clock face was re-gilded and the carving over the church door cleaned and repaired. The cost was £15000 and an appeal was launched in 1996 to raise the money. A number of events were organised including social evenings, whist drives and a church open weekend, with tours of the tower itself. But most popular were the visits to parishioners' gardens in the summer. Verdant Stoke Bishop rose to the occasion with twenty six homes opening their gardens. The idea lingered on, but it was cream teas as much as the gardens that became the attraction.

Below ground the boiler was wearing out. It was costly to run and could not always be relied upon to heat the church adequately. In 1998 it was replaced by a modern gas fired boiler that was in every way more efficient. It was fully automatic, had twice the output and could heat the church in one hour from cold.

The church rooms also enjoyed a 'make-over'. Anyone who joined the throng in the main hall after the 9.45 service often had difficulties making themselves heard. The solution was to lower the ceiling and lay carpet tiles. Softer lighting was installed at the same time. The effect was striking, an altogether more relaxing ambience in which to enjoy after service coffee. The work was paid for from the Goodbody legacy, given by a long time member of the congregation, Margaret Goodbody. In tribute to her generosity the PCC named the small room off the main hall after her.

Office Changes

When David Ritchie arrived he inherited a secretary working part time and the tiny Goodbody room as an office. With the arrival of the church manager resources and accommodation were clearly inadequate. The PCC approved the plan to transfer the office to the much larger Wright room between the church and the church rooms. This provided easier and more direct access from the road. The playgroup no longer had visitors stumbling over small children on their way to the office. A further change came when the local authority introduced new rules regarding the conduct of the playgroup and stipulated that it be sealed off from all contact with the public. As the Goodbody room was being used at the time as additional office space, the church manager, Roy Percy, who had taken over from Mike Barwell, and was now employed full time, suggested that the Wright room be re-designed to create two smaller offices, an inner one for the main administration and an outer one where visitors could call. Further improvements were effected with the carpeting of the steps from the church and the lobby area. This more welcoming environment was further enhanced by an information desk and the main bookstall, racked with brightly coloured paperbacks.

Alongside these structural changes came the installation of equipment which gradually modernised the communications of the church. It began, at the start of the interregnum, with the arrival of an answering machine. When David Ritchie came his mobility in the services was helped by the purchase of a radio microphone - no more plugging in and being restrained by an umbilical wire. Computers and a sophisticated photo-copier allowed the church to cut its costs and do much more printing from the office. A desk top publishing package freed the magazine editor from the monthly visit to the printer to create the layout. Now all the publishing could be done ‘in house’. A fax machine, more elaborate soft-ware, a colour printer and scanner, e-mail were one by one added to the armoury of the office.

Finance

Most of the costs for the refurbishment and new equipment were borne by gifts and legacies. The value of these was continually stressed by the treasurer and a number of initiatives were made to persuade people of the benefits of giving in this way, particularly as the return from covenants was being eroded by the reductions in income tax. A one off addition to the church's income came in 1997. when the PCC agreed to sell the curate's house at 7, Little Stoke Road and invest the proceeds, there being no likely need for it in the future. The sale came at a time when the two great outgoings were staff salaries and the diocesan quota. The irony did not escape the finance committee that whereas St Mary's once had a curate paid for by the diocese, it now not only had an increase in quota, but had to pay for any staff to make up for the lack of a curate out of its own pocket. There were rumblings about with-holding part of the quota, but Christine Froude, herself non-stipendary, argued "that without the financial help from parishes such as St Mary's, it would be impossible to maintain the ministry of the church in the socially deprived areas of our city and diocese...... There are no high priests or Roman governors or legions of soldiers in Knowle West or Southmead, Withywood or Hartcliffe, but there is poverty, prostitution, drug abuse, alcoholism, unemployment, family breakdown, evils in people's lives and injuries within society that need to be illuminated by the light of the gospel." It was a persuasive argument, but in August 1999, when Christine Froude, after four years at St Mary's, took up a new post as locum chaplain at the Bristol Royal Infirmary and Bristol General Hospital, the perceived burden of the quota re-emerged.

Vision

In all the scrambling to acquire ever more effective means of communication, the clergy found it necessary to stop and ask what it was exactly that they were wanting to communicate. At the PCC Away Day in 1997, held in the hall of Redland Parish Church, this pause for thought produced a vision for St Mary's based around the fundamental question: "why do we exist as a church?" "Churches," explained the vicar, "with a clear and well publicised vision statement, which they use to order their priorities and measure their achievements, are growing with a real sense of direction and purpose." The idea, borrowed from the world of corporate business, was enthusiastically embraced by the PCC and together with the clergy the members hammered out a statement that was launched in the January of the following year. In the form of a prayer it embraced a vision for the future:

> *"Heavenly Father, may we become a living community of Christ's people, each one of us bound together in his love and in commitment to one another, in order to be equipped and led by the Holy Spirit to serve Christ in the parish and in the world, for the glory of His name. Amen."*

To accompany the vision statement, ten core values were identified which it was felt were central to the life of St Mary's and which were the practical expression of the vision. These were explained in the magazine, discussed in house groups and proclaimed on banners around the church. To mark a new beginning a logo was designed which appeared on all St Mary's publications. It represented the church within a radiant seed head, with the wind of God's spirit dispersing the seeds throughout the parish and beyond (it can be seen on the back cover of this book.). The message was delivered to every home in the parish through the Messenger. This thrice yearly newsletter had evolved from the annual cards with their seasonal messages that were traditionally delivered around the parish at Christmas and Easter. It was launched in 1995 and was produced in tabloid form using pictures, stories and cartoons in journalistic style to explain St Mary's to the non-churchgoer.

Mission and Outreach

One characteristic of this period was the shift from evening to daytime activities, particularly those involving women. More and more women went out to work, and after a busy day were less inclined to go out in the evening, even when they considered it safe to do so. Groups like the Mother's Union and Wives Fellowship (or Tuesday Fellowship as it was later called), which were formed when women had more time at their disposal, no longer met at St Mary's. But during the day there was a growing number of opportunities for mothers with young children to meet. Mums and tots and the pre-school playgroup continued to thrive. Open House was a weekly meeting of fellowship, discussion and bible study. The brain child of Lis Ritchie, the vicar's wife, it met in the vicarage with an attendant creche and quickly attracted a number of mothers at home with small children.

Alongside this growing outreach was an equal concern to ensure adequate protection for children while in the church's care. The diocese made it clear churches had to be on their guard against possible abuse of children in their midst even though to many such a possibility seemed incredible. New procedures of vetting were introduced that were designed not only to ensure the safety of children, but also to protect the many who worked with them. Essential though the new policy was, it put an added strain on the church's resources, as no child could now be left in the care of a single adult.

St Mary's continued to support a number of missions and individuals overseas, including Sue Woodcock in Bolivia and later Spain, Colin and Anne Chapman in Beirut and Lucy Monk, the daughter of a former St Mary's curate, in central Asia. Korky Davey's work continued to find new openings and, dramatically in 1999, he and his team were instrumental in helping a number of refugees from the Kosovo conflict re-habilitate themselves. On the home front homelessness and drug abuse were two particular areas of concern which translated into practical help. Several members of St Mary's were actively involved with the Crisis Centre in the inner city area of St Paul's. This ran a café for those on the streets and issued meal vouchers which people bought and gave to anyone they found begging on the pavement. That person could then exchange the voucher for a hot meal at the Crisis Centre café. Another practical expression of help was the monthly collection of food tins which were distributed to the needy by the Sisters of the Church in St Paul's. But perhaps the greatest achievement of these years - and history must judge whether this was so - was the renewal that was felt in the church when it decided to run an Alpha course in September 1996.

David Ritchie launches St Mary's vision statement in1998

Christine Froude, St Mary's first woman priest, at a Pets Service on the Downs in 1998

Alpha, Beta, Gamma ......

Alpha was a phenomenon of the nineties. It was a revivalist movement that began at Holy Trinity church, Brompton, in West London. The latter caught the headlines through its reputation as a 'yuppies' church, but it was much more than that. It touched a raw nerve of the post-Christian era in which Britain now found itself. Many were growing up ignorant of the basic truth of Christianity but feeling there was something missing in their lives. In the words of Sandy Millar, vicar of Holy Trinity, "stripping the gospel down to its bare essentials makes Christianity accessible to men and women of today's culture." A ten week course was constructed whose reputation travelled by word of mouth. It was taken up by churches nation-wide and across all denominations. By the time St Mary's decided to run a course thousands had already done so.

It was a shrewd package. At its heart were two elements, a meal and a video. The evening began with a hot supper, which allowed everyone to relax and get to know each other. The video that followed was a well crafted presentation by Nicky Gumbell, the curate at Holy Trinity, of an aspect of the gospel which he expounded with clarity and humour. Dressed with designer informality, his pleasing personality had an instant appeal as he tackled questions like 'who is Jesus?', 'why did he die?', 'does God heal today?'. The evening ended with a gloves off discussion of the issues raised.

The first course at St Mary's got off to a flying start - literally, with the vicar's supply of parrot jokes seeming inexhaustible. It was fully subscribed as indeed was the next one after Christmas. In the first instance most of those attending already came to church, but many found it a chance to strengthen their faith and recharge their spiritual batteries. Groups bonded and the cement hardened further with the Away Day, which was an integral part of the course. As one person wrote: "I am getting to know more people. Although I have been a member of St Mary's for at least 48 years there are many, many people I do not know." Another: "I have discovered something that now fills the gap that has been in my life since childhood."

To run a course of this kind demanded an army of people. The whole church found itself involved. House groups provided the food, cooked to Alpha recipes, and brought hot to the church hall in foil containers. Teams were recruited to lay out the tables and clear up afterwards, to operate the sound and vision, to host and lead the discussions. By the time the fifth course was being run in the autumn of 1997 it was estimated that 2000 meals had been cooked and of those who were currently attending 30-40% had no previous connection with the church. To build on the foundation laid by Alpha, a number of nurturing, or Beta courses, were started, leading to a further course of Christian growth, the Gamma. No one, least of all David Ritchie, had underestimated the difficulties of these last years, but the experience of Alpha had enriched lives and given the church the renewed hope that it could move confidently into the second millennium.

Appendix 1

Vicars

David Wright 1860-95

Second son of Job Wright, gentleman, of St Lawrence Jewry, London. Magdalen Hall, Oxford, 1840. Curate St John's, Redland. Vicar, Stoke Bishop 1860. Minor Canon, Bristol Cathedral 1849-60. Died 1896.

Josiah Alford 1895-1909

Second son of Charles Alford, Bishop of Victoria, Hong Kong. Curate, St Leonards 1870-1. Curate, Cleeve, Somerset 1871-3. Minor Canon, Bristol Cathedral 1873-81. Vicar, St Nicholas with St Leonard, Bristol 1880-95. Vicar, Stoke Bishop 1895-1909. Hon. Canon, Bristol Cathedral 1897-1912. Canon, Bristol Cathedral 1912-24. Rural Dean, Stapleton 1905-11. Commissary to Archdeacon of Brisbane 1912-21. C.B.E. 1919. Chaplain, 1st Division, Southern Command, 1914-18 War. Died 1924.

Alfred Clifford 1910-21

Curate, St Nicholas, Nottingham 1872-4. C.M.S. missionary to India, Calcutta 1874-9, Krishnagar, 1879-85. Chaplain to Metropolitan Bishop 1885. C.M.S. Secretary in Calcutta 1886-92. First Bishop of Lucknow 1893-1911. Vicar, Stoke Bishop 1910-21. Retired. Died 27 April 1931.

Sydney Worters 1936-49

Trinity College, Cambridge. Curate, Sherston Magna, Wiltshire 1902-6. Curate, Stratton St Margaret, Swindon 1906-9. Rector, Luckington, Wiltshire 1909-12. Curate, St Michael's and All Angels, Bishopston, Bristol 1912-16. Vicar, Oldland 1917-22. Vicar, St Luke's, Brislington 1922-36. Rural Dean, Bedminster 1928-36. Vicar, Stoke Bishop 1936-49. Hon. Chaplain, Bishop of Bristol 1946-53. Rector, Winterbourne 1949-53.

Henry Bothamley 1949-54

Magdalen College, Oxford. Curate, St Paul's, Onslow Square, London 1921-4. Curate, St James's, Paddington 1925-6. Vicar, St Mary with St

John, Harlow 1926-36. Rural Dean, Harlow 1935-6. Vicar, Clifton 1936-49. Rural Dean, Clifton 1940-54. Hon. Canon, Bristol Cathedral 1946-54. Vicar, Stoke Bishop 1949-54. Vicar, Taunton 1954-60. Vicar Leigh Woods, Bristol 1960-68. Died 1976.

Norman Hulbert 1955-60

Bristol University. Curate, St Saviour's, Woolcott Park 1930-2. Curate, St James with St John the Baptist 1932-6. Priest-in-charge, St Barnabas, Knowle, Bristol 1936-44. Vicar, St Luke's, Brislington 1944-55. Rural Dean, Bedminster 1949-55. Vicar, Stoke Bishop 1955-1960. Died 1960.

Leslie Williams 1960-1967

Born 1909. Clifton Theological College 1934. Curate, Holy Trinity, Bristol 1934-7. Cambridge BA History & Theology 1937-40. Curate, Chippenham 1940-2. Chaplain L.A.F.V.R. 1942-46. Curate, Stoke Bishop 1946-7. Vicar, Corsham 1947-52. Vicar, Bishopston 1952-60. Vicar, Stoke Bishop 1960-1967. Archdeacon, Bristol 1967-79. Lord Mayor's chaplain 1968-96. Died 1996.

Roy Henderson 1968-1992

Born 1927. Braesnose College, Oxford 1948-51. MA Geography. Ridley College, Cambridge 1952-54. Curate, St Leonard's, Exeter1954-57. Travelling secretary, Inter-Varsity Fellowship 1957-60. Vicar, St Luke with Christ Church, Barton Hill, Bristol 1960-68. Priest-in-charge, St Philip and St Jacob 1967-68. Vicar, Stoke Bishop 1968-92. Lecturer, Clifton/Trinity Theological College, 1969-73. Rural Dean, Westbury and Severnside Deanery 1973-79. Hon. Canon, Bristol Cathedral 1980-1992. Hon. Canon Emeritus, Bristol Cathedral 1992.

David Ritchie 1993 -

Born 1948. St John's College, Durham 1972-74. BA & Dip. Theology. Curate, Harold Wood, Chelmsford, 1974-79. Team vicar, Ipsley, Worcester, 1979-84. Chaplain, Vevey, D'Oex, Villars, Switzerland. Council of Intercontinental Church Society. Vicar, Stoke Bishop 1993 -

Appendix 2

Assistant Curates

Donald Maclean Claxton	1875-79
William Oldham	1880-82
William Boyd	1882-84
Patrick Watson	1883-85
Herbert Awdry Mais	1887-90
Ernest Alfred Browne	1890-94
John Bright	1894-95
Thomas Charles Clark	1895-02
Curling Finzel Doddrell	1902-05
Frederick Rogers	1905-06
Reginald Jeffcoat	1906-10
Ralph Layard Whytehead	1910-15
Frederick Richard Henry Crews	1915-17
Ralph Layard Whytehead	1919-22
Frank Mason Hookham	1923-27
Percival Strettall Chadwick	1928-36
Henry Richard Radcliffe Cock	1936-38
Ronald Austin Cowling	1938-40
John Ford	1940-42
David Rufus Price	1941-43
Stephen Seel Sherwood Swindells	1944-46
Leslie Arthur Williams	1946-47
Richard Roderick Poole	1948
Leonard Golledge	1948-49
John Richard Lyn Scammell	1950-53
John Capenhurst Burnett	1953-56
Bernard Herbert Vincent Brown	1956-59
David Henry Sansum	1960-64
Alan Charles Dowsett	1964-67
Nicholas John Monk	1967-69
Barry John Morrison	1969-72

William Richard Kew	1972-76
Reginald Leslie Bell (NSM)	1974-75
Charles Michael Blunsum (NSM)	1974-79
Andrew Daunton-Fear	1976-79
William George Challis	1979-82
Philip Dixon	1982-84
Richard Alexander Lyon Welby	1984-88
Stewart William Jones	1988-92
James Maxwell Rex (NSM)	1989-91
Christine Ann Froude	1995-99

Appendix 3

Churchwardens

There is no complete list of churchwardens available for the early years, but the following information appeared in an earlier history of St Mary Magdalene by Ronald Warne.

The first churchwardens were J. Battersby Harford and T. Terrett Taylor who served for 20 years.
The following were known to have served between 1880 and 1925

J. Godwin
J. C. Godwin
A. Lewis (1901)
G. Lane (1901)
T. Fletcher (1908)
H.V. Barnard (1908)
G.H. Perrin
H.H.Townsend
J.F.Jacques
Meade King
P. Lindrea
W. H. Watkins
G. Budgett (1922)
H. R. Smith (1922)
Colonel F. C. S. Norrington

From 1925

Colonel F. C. S. Norrington	1925-36
W. E. Budgett	1925-26
T. F. Miller	1926-29
C. L. Belden	1929-32
J. Hill	1932-40
C. J. Sansbury	1936-39
Dr Robin Brocklehurst	1939-60
G. King	1940-41

Dr C.C. Lavington	1941-44
Harry Shawcross	1944-45
Dr C.C. Lavington	1945-46
W.G. Pelmear	1946-49
Harry Shawcross	1949-53
E. Bland	1953-58
Tom Barr	1958-62
George Sisman	1960
Arthur Carter	1960-63
Frank Evans	1962-65
Ronald Warne	1963-66
W. G. Purnell	1965-68
Tom Cutter	1966-69
R. A. Chermside	1968-71
Ralph Vincent	1969-72
Major Rodney Patey	1971-74
George Sisman	1972-74
Frank Coward	1974-76
Dr Martin Halford	1974-78
Harry Raiss	1976-79
Bill Burkett	1978-81
Adrian Codrington	1979-80
Malcolm Barnett	1980-83
Paul Parnell	1981-84
Don Hore	1983-86
John Rosser	1984-85
John Davis	1985-88
Margaret Sellin	1986-89
Keith Sheather	1988-91
Jenny Baker	1989-92
Dr David Speedyman	1991-94
Mary Burkett	1992-95
George Smith	1994-97
Mary Parnell	1995-98
Christopher Smith	1997-
Judith Sheather	1998-

Appendix 4

Occupation of fathers from the Baptismal Registers 1905-1914

Gardeners	17	Farm Labourers	2
Coachmen	9	Shepherd	1
Chauffeurs	6	Labourers	2
Servants	3	Carter	1
		Plate Layer	1

Directors	2
Army Officers	2
Surgeon	1
Architect	1
Solicitors	2
Accountant	1
Gentlemen	2

Sgts. Police and Army	2	Merchants	2
Station Masters	2	Coal Merchants	2
GWR Guard	1	Corn Merchant	1
Grocer	1	Wholesale Clothier	1
Baker	1	Manufacturers	2
Dairymen	2	Engineers	2
Postman	1	Brewer	1
Stone Masons	2	Contractor	1
Carpenter	1	Assayer	1
Motor Mechanic	1	Civil Servant	1
Clerks	2	Land Agent's Assistant	1
Insurance Agent	1	Organist	1
Pensioner	1	Unmarried Mothers	2

Appendix 5

Occupation of fathers from the Baptismal Registers 1958-59

Directors	8	Van Driver	1
Ship Owner	1	Hall Porter	1
Managers	11	Joiner	1
Company Reps	10	Mechanic	1
Doctors	4	Civil Servants	6
Engineers	8	Local Government	3
Accountants	3	Gardener	1
Surveyors	3	Factory Inspector	1
Clergymen	2	Pharmacist	1
Architect	1	Bank Official	1
Chartered Secretary	1	Buyer	1
Solicitor	1	Agents	2
Stock Broker	1	Law Stationer	1
Schoolmaster	1	Tarpaulin manufacturer	1
University Lecturer	1	Sub-postmaster	1
Research Chemist	1	Electrician	1
Metallurgists	2	Fishmonger	1
Geophysical Explorer	1	Students	2
Company Registrar	1	Unmarried mother	1

Appendix 6

Occupation of fathers from the Baptismal Register 1998

Chartered Accountant
Data Manager
Computer Business Consultant
Sales Manager
Chartered Surveyor
Teacher
Chef
Surgeon
Financial Adviser
Company Director (2)
Marketing Director (3)
Software Engineer
General Practitioner
Civil Servant (2)
Bank Clerk
Builder
Student
Photographer

Appendix 7

Statement of Accounts for 1926

Expenditure

	£	s	p
Stipend to vicar	600	--	--
Stipend to curate	300	--	--
Less contributions to clergy fund	232	17	6
	667	2	6
Easter offering to vicar	79	17	7
Choir and music	89	7	6
Organist	75	--	--
Organ tuning	8	8	--
Taxis for choir	8	2	--
Less contribution for choir fund	54	11	--
	126	6	--
Salary of verger	100	--	--
Cleaning and washing materials etc	7	19	11
Fuel	24	17	6
Electricity, gas and water	20	19	2
Repairs Organ	17	16	--
Roof	11	5	8
Boiler	9	10	--
Printing	38	11	8
Insurance	10	12	7
Bank charges and cheque book	4	12	5
Sundries including hassocks, wine, stamps etc	12	10	2
	1118	**11**	**--**

Receipts

	£	s	p
Offertories	480	17	4
Pew rents	428	16	--
Easter Offering	79	19	7

Special contributions	**£**	**s**	**p**
Churchyard	4	4	--
School treat	2	2	--
Deficit for the year	6	6	--
	1118	**11**	**--**

Additional special collections:

St Thomas, Eastville	10	5	--
Poor parishes of Bristol	52	11	3
Church Missionary Society	12	5	1
Diocesan Refuge	9	10	--
Church Mission to the Jews	6	5	3
Missions to Seamen	11	19	10
Society for the Propagation of the Gospel	15	10	2
Society for the Propagation of Christian Knowledge	13	12	9
Church of England Men's Society	2	2	--
Hospitals	31	14	8
Bristol Clergy Fund	10	10	--
Assistant Curates Society	6	1	3

Bibliographical Note

The two published works which provided much useful material for the early chapters are:

Memorials of Stoke Bishop
- David Wright (1897) *pub. John Wright & Co., Bristol*

The Story of St Mary Magdalene, 1858-1958
- Ronald Frederick Warne (1959) *privately published*

A more general history of the area is to be found in:

A Pictorial History of Stoke Bishop and Sneyd Park
- compiled by Penny Jetzer, Diana Bourne, Elizabeth Floyd and Monica Carp and published by the Stoke Bishop and Sneyd Park Local History Group (1998)

The Parish Magazines were an invaluable source of information. These have survived from 1940.

Unpublished documents consulted and lodged in the Bristol Record Office include:

Harford Family Papers (28048)
Bristol Diocesan Records (EP)

The Bristol Record Office holds a range of papers relating to St Mary's catalogued as follows:

P/St. MSB/I	Incumbent
P/St. MSB/ChW	Churchwardens
P/St. MSB/V	Vestry
P/St. MSB/PCC	Parochial Church Council
P/St. MSB/Sch	School
P/St. MSB/Soc	Societies
P/St. MSB/P	Maps and plans
P/St. MSB/PM	Printed material